CARRICK

SCOTLAND

Beyond the tourist guides

JAMES BROWN

Line drawings by Beryl Dawdry

HISTORY ❖ GEOLOGY ❖ FLORA ❖ FAUNA

"We think na on the lang Scots miles ...."

Published on behalf of Carrick Community Councils' Forum by Ailsa Horizons Ltd
Registered in Scotland No: SC327632
Recognised Scottish Charity: SC 038211

ISBN: 978-0-9563061-0-4

Printed in Scotland by Walker & Connel Ltd
Hastings Square, Darvel, Ayrshire

Carrick Community Councils' Forum gratefully acknowledges the financial support of the Heritage Lottery Fund and Hadyard Hill Community Benefit Fund Ltd in the production of this book.

CONTENTS

Seal of Duncan,
Earl of Carrick
c.1250

Detail of a map of
Scotland by
Abraham Ortelius 1573
with west at the top.

Tectonic plate movement diagram from *Girvan Fossils* by Mark Hope, 2001, published by the McKechnie Institute, Girvan.

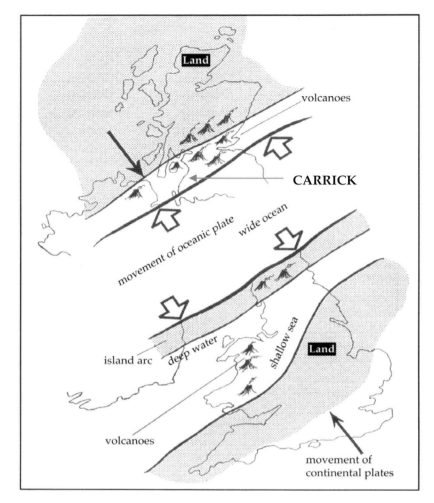

Elizabeth Gray
(1831-1924) daughter of an innkeeper who had a self-taught interest in fossils. Mrs Gray took up the passion and collected fossils into her tenth decade.

Alexander McCallum
(1802-1854)
Known as *Lang Sandy*, a *lad o pairts* whose dedication and persistence in learning about, and finding, fossils earned him a lasting reputation which was acknowledged in the book, *On the Silurian Rocks of the South of Scotland* by Sir Roderick Murchison (1792-1871).

1 TECTONIC PLATES & VOLCANOES

"A volcano is not made on purpose to frighten superstitious people into fits of piety and devotion, nor to overwhelm devoted cities with destruction; a volcano should be considered as a spiracle to the subterranean furnace, in order to prevent the unnecessary elevation of land, and fatal effects of earthquakes..."

James Hutton (1726 – 1797), founder of modern geology, *Theory of the Earth*, 1785

The mainland of Scotland has long been described geologically as Highlands, Central Lowlands (or Midland Valley) and Southern Uplands with two major fault lines creating obvious divisions. Carrick, a complex area of hills and valleys lies in the south-western part of the Lowlands. A series of lesser fault lines running from south-west to north east have created small-scale river valleys and ridgelines.

Fossil of the Upper Ordovician period *Calymene drummuckensis* named after Drummuck near Girvan.

This green and fertile land, bordered on the west by the sheltered waters of the Firth of Clyde, presents a picture of rural tranquillity. To the east of Dailly, Barr and Barrhill stands the western part of the Southern Uplands. Benign rolling hills shelter picturesque villages. But the hills and gentle river valleys of the Duisk, Stinchar and Water of Girvan yield clues to the cataclysmic turmoil the country we now know as Scotland went through.

Clashes between Scotland and England are literally as old as the hills. About 500 million years ago the American and European continents drifted towards each other, slowly closing a 5,000 km (3,125 mile) gap. The Earth's crust, is split into enormous sections known as tectonic plates, moved in a process called subduction whereby the dense oceanic crust slid under the lighter continental crust. That wide ancient ocean shrank over a period of 70 million years and the rocks which formed what is now England, Wales and southern Ireland joined the American continent where the rocks of Scotland lay. The collision is known as the Caledonian Orogeny.

The evidence for this can be found in the profusion of fossilised trilobites found in Scotland and England. These little creatures which look like woodlice (or slaters as they are known in Scotland) are totally different on either side of the Border. It is believed that the vast ocean that originally separated the countries was too wide for them to cross, hence their different development.

The Ballantrae Complex

Pillow lava

Since the mid-19th century the origin of this very interesting geological area has been a source of study, debate and speculation by some of the most eminent geologists. In the 1970s it was concluded that it is an obducted ophiolite complex. That is, it is a fragment of ocean crust and underlying mantle that had been forced up on to the continental landmass instead of being drawn down with the rest of the ocean plate.

The complex extends to perhaps 40-50 km (25-30 miles) in depth. But outcrops along the coast between Girvan and Ballantrae such as at Kennedy's Pass as well as exposed areas on higher ground inland offer plenty of opportunities for accessible study of the complex's main components of pillow lavas, cherts, lava conglomerates and fossil-rich shales. In addition there are shallow-marine limestones and deep-water greywackes. These represent rocks from various levels in the Earth's crust.

Not all geological mysteries have been solved, though, and that is the great attraction of the Girvan area. There is an abundance of highly significant problems that remain unresolved which has brought a steady stream of geologists to the region for the past 100 years or so.

Volcanoes

As a result of subduction the melting crust formed magma chambers: enormous pools of molten rocks, ash and gasses which fed the volcanoes. As these cooled between 400 and 500 million years ago, granites were formed which can now be found in various parts of Carrick, most famously on Ailsa Craig. The process of the magma cooling inside the Earth created intrusive igneous rocks such as gabbro and granite. Extrusive igneous rocks, such as basalt and andesite, formed at the Earth's surface and are common in the west coast of Scotland. They are particular evident in Carrick. Many of the extrusive rock types are also found as thin intrusive bodies called dykes and sills.

Volcanoes are extinct in Scotland as the country is no longer close to a tectonic plate boundary. But traces of them remain in many places. They support the castles of Stirling and Edinburgh. and Arthur's Seat, at the other end of Edinburgh's Royal Mile is another landmark example. About one mile from Maybole is Mochrum Hill, a volcanic plug which was part of a very large volcano. Evidence of the volcanic activity is found at the nearby Brown Carrick Hill and Maybole Shore at Dunure. This former fishing village is famous for its agates.

The great forces that formed Carrick subsided millions of years ago. Since then the evolution of flora, fauna and human intervention has created the landscape we see today. Change continues, often imperceptibly. The area is not immune from global climatic changes so the subtle variations in plants and wildlife happen alongside the arrival of new technology to meet the need for sustainable energy resources.

Hadyard Hill, near Dailly   © Fred Westcott

2 FOSSILS & COLLECTORS

I employed myself in searching for fossil bones;
this point being a perfect catacomb for monsters of extinct races.

Charles Darwin (1809-1882) in his account of the voyage of the *Beagle* in 1839

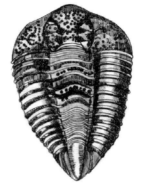

An almost perfect trilobite fossil found at Drummuck by Girvan.

James Hutton, founder of modern geology, by John Kay, Edinburgh

In Carrick there is no need to sail to faraway places in search of fossils, for the region is a geologist's dream, and a perplexing one too. The great and complicated Silurian rocks in the Girvan area have puzzled experts for nearly two centuries. The movement of the earth's tectonic plates created a unique phenomenon: as one plate sank below another the former folded back on itself leaving us with a vast treasure of fossilised corals, starfish and trilobites. Although all manner of flora and fauna has been fossilised, it is the oceanic evidence that has justly made Carrick world-famous.

The largest trilobite fossil found in the United Kingdom was from this area. With such a fabulous hoard of fossil remains it is no surprise that Girvan should produce one of the most famous and remarkable collectors in the country. Elizabeth Gray (1831-1924), the youngest daughter of Thomas and Mary Anderson, was born in the Burns Arms Inn, Alloway. In 1836 the family moved to Girvan when her father gave up innkeeping to become a farmer. With a keen interest in fossils, he collected those exposed in local roadstone quarries.

In an 1897 academic paper by the geologists Nicholson and Etheridge, a trilobite - *Bronteus andersoni* - was dedicated by them '*to this intelligent and enthusiastic collector*' and they later named a coral after him. Distinguished geologist Dr Francis Bather (1863-1934) named two fossils after Anderson's daughter: *Cothurnocystis elizae* and *Aulechinus grayae*.

Elizabeth's own interest in fossils continued after her marriage in 1856 to a Glasgow banker, Robert Gray, who assisted her fossil collecting. She amassed over 30,000 specimens, actively searching to within a few months of her death at the age of 92. Her first collection was donated to the Hunterian Museum in the University of Glasgow in 1866 and others were given to the Sedgwick Museum in Cambridge. A later, larger collection was sold to the Natural History Museum in London.

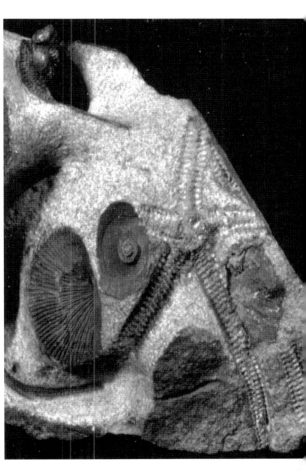

Girvan fossils

Carrick has fascinated geologists. In the first half of the 19th century the great geologist and writer, Hugh Miller (1802-1856), of Cromarty in north-east Scotland, made several visits to Carrick. His local guide was another self-taught enthusiast, Alexander McCallum (1804-1854) of Girvan. *Lang Sandy*, as he was known, was a tall, strong man who travelled extensively in Carrick in pursuit of his deep passion for geology. His earlier subsistence occupations of weaver and occasional fisherman gave way to his making a living as a collector of fossils and antiquities and, of course, as a highly knowledgeable guide to visiting geologists such as Miller. Sadly he died in poverty, of cholera. The fate of his collections is unknown but it is probable that they were sold to provide for his large family.

Although most attention has been focused on Girvan fossils, significant finds have been made further inland around the villages of Barr and Barrhill. But the heyday of fossil collecting is long gone although finds continue to be made, often by amateurs, in small, roadside quarries and on the foreshore (at low tide) a few miles south of Girvan. The Ordovician fossils found there tend to be fragmentary.

To the untrained eye, one trilobite may look very much like another. But there are many varieties, some were blind, others had eyes on stalks. The Girvan area has yielded a number of species, often as complete specimens. This humble, bizarre little creature is not the only ocean dweller to be found of course. A wide variety of shells remains in abundance, some of them resembling the familiar snails, whelks, cockles and mussels of today.

The most charming survivors from over 400 million years ago must surely be the starfish. Around 20 species from two localities in the Girvan area have been found and most of these are tiny – around 1 cm across. The Girvan specimens are among the oldest in the world, as are the rare finds of primitive sea-urchins.

Visitors to the long coastline of Carrick are captivated by the spectacular profile of Arran and Holy Isle and the distinctive bulk of Ailsa Craig. Perhaps occasionally they should turn their gaze to the fascinating rock formations and wide sandy beaches, for there lays not *buried* treasure, but traces of our ancient past such as an observant beachcomber at Maidens discovered – colourful fossilised coral.

Dunure agates and agatised coral (*below, left*)

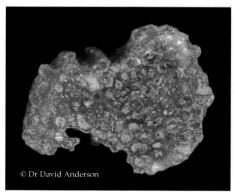

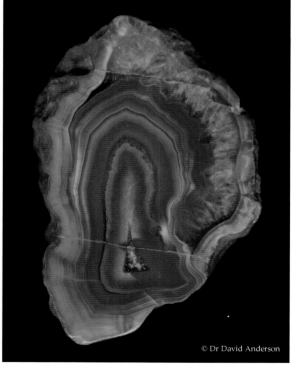

3 REMAINS TO BE SEEN

"It was in Scotland that I acquired precision in my ideas regarding ancient glaciers. The existence in that country of so considerable a network of these traces enabled me to appreciate better the geological mechanism of glaciers and the importance of many facts of detail observed in the neighbourhood of those which now exist."

Louis Agassiz (1807-1873), the Swiss geologist who first developed the idea of continental-scale glaciation, writing two years after a tour of the west Highlands in 1840 where he first tested his theories.

Eroded rocks at **Croy** beach, like an abstract work of art

The clashing continents and exploding cauldrons of magma which created rocky Carrick millions of years ago were followed by the crushing, carving forces of vast ice sheets. Over the millennia ice ages have come and gone with the last major one in Scotland peaking around 18,000 years ago. A layer of ice more than 1 km thick flowed across the country, gouging out U-shaped valleys, reducing mountains and depositing material which can still be seen today as scattered boulders and large chunks of rock, hundreds of kilometres from their source.

Dunure Castle

The massive weight of the ice cap pushed the country down. But after it had melted about 10,000 years ago, the land very slowly began to rise back up, a process that continues today. In Carrick we see the evidence in the distinctive and impressive raised beaches at numerous locations including Greenan, Bracken Bay (by the Heads of Ayr), Dunure, Culzean Harbour and Turnberry Point. Further south, there are raised beaches at Dipple, Carleton and at The Whilk, 1.6 km (one mile) south-west of Lendalfoot, where former sea stacks of dolerite can be seen. Either side of Ballantrae there are examples at Corseclays and where the River Stinchar enters the Firth of Clyde.

Pillow lavas

Although the majority of the volcanic evidence is now buried under forests, soils and settlements, the shoreline remains a window on the past. Perhaps the most entrancing are the pillow lavas. These were formed when the lava flows emerged under water and quickly cooled, creating a thin, glassy crust around a bulbous mass of lava. As pressure built, the lava burst out to form a pillow shape. Each time new "pillows" formed, they piled up and sagged against each other. It only happened with lavas of a basaltic composition.

Examples from the late Ordovician period (490-443 million years ago) can be seen at Downan Point, south of Ballantrae. They are the finest examples of this feature in the United Kingdom. Rapid cooling of many of the Ballantrae pillows caused violent fragmentation, leaving thick beds of volcanic debris among the lavas. To the south of Culzean Harbour slipway a low wall of vesicular andesite has a strongly pillowed base with individual pillows up to two metres across. *Vesicular* describes the numerous small cavities which are a result of gas bubbles in the lava. The andesites from this site have been described by distinguished geologist, Alexander Geikie (1835-1924) as some of the most beautiful volcanic rocks in Scotland. This location is also noted for the veins and masses of agate and quartz. Cliffs of andesite lava can be seen inland, rising above the alluvium-covered flood plain of the Water of Girvan at Craig Hill, 4 km (2.5 miles) south-south-east of the beautiful village of Straiton.

Agates

These attractive by-products of volcanic activity can be found in many countries around the world. Scotland has comparatively few but the variety of colour, pattern and beauty marks them out as special. They are quartz nodules found within other rocks and form within cavities of volcanic rock. But the exact process is complex and not fully understood. When the nodules are sliced open they reveal spectacular natural art with infinitely varied patterns and colours. Most agates are basically red and blue but the range of shades is considerable.

Finds can still be made on beaches along the coast from Heads of Ayr to Turnberry in lavas of the Devonian Period (417-354 million years ago) but they are becoming rare due to their past reputation and ease of access. Other places where agates are found are ploughed fields and cliffs.

Flaggy sandstones

For sheer geological drama, mention must be made of Ardwell Bay, just south of Girvan, where convoluted and contorted strata of sandstone, siltstone and mudstone appear to sway in harmony with the waves and offshore breezes. It is a beguiling place not only for geologists and fossil collectors, but for artists and photographers.

Serpentinite

This rare stone is the result of a process of change in rocks rich in minerals which are not stable on the Earth's surface. The resultant red, green and brown patterns which run through it are thought to resemble snake skin, hence the name. Being relatively soft, it is rarely exposed and at the coast it tends to be buried beneath a raised beach. The Ballantrae Complex which consists of bands of serpentinite, lava and abundant igneous intrusions generally of gabbro and dolerite, has in its northern section, a serpentinite belt 1.5 km wide, stretching over 11 km (7 miles) from Burnfoot to Byne Hill near Girvan.

Ardwell Bay

4 AILSA CRAIG

"Northwart fra this Isle of Man 60 miles of sea lyes Ellsay an Isle of ane mile lang, quharin is ane greit heich hill round and roche, and als abundant of Solan-geese, and ane small point of ane Ness quhairat the Fisher-boats lyes: for the same Isle is very good for fishing, sic as Keiling, Ling and other white fishes. Forenent this Isle lyes Carrick on the south-east part, and the Lands of Kintyre on the west and north-west part; the said Ellsay being marchand midsea betwixt the said Marches."

A Descriptioune of the Western Iles of Scotland called Hybrides, Compiled by **Mr Donald Munro**, Deane of the Iles, 1549

Curling stones are still made of Ailsa granite, in Mauchline, Ayrshire.

A small, precipitous, uninhabited island it may be, but Ailsa Craig has made its mark on the world. The reasons are many and eclectic. It is famous for pirates, volcanoes, curling stones, an inland parish with a lighthouse, a vast bird colony, the 'delicacy' of solan geese, a castle, an ancient chapel, an actress's stage name, an innovative taxidermist, written accounts by many geologists, naturalists and travellers, a landmark for the Irish, a backdrop to world-famous golf, a Marquis's title, a John Keats sonnet, a poem by William Wordsworth, and one solitary mention by Scotland's national bard, the Ayrshire poet, Robert Burns.

Detail from Timothy Pont's map of Arran c.1590s; note the castle, and the anchor to indicate a harbour

Ailza

This iconic, dome-shaped island, 15 km (9.5 miles) west of Girvan is also famous for something it is not; an extinct volcano. Certainly it is the result of volcanic action and in geological terms is an igneous intrusion composed of microgranite of the Palaeogene age (formed between 60 and 55 million years ago). This distinctive blue-grey rock is characterised by alkali pyroxene and amphibole minerals, particularly aegerine and arfedsonite. The island is important as peralkaline rocks of this composition are relatively rare in the Scottish Tertiary volcanic province, the youngest of the country's solid rocks. Glaciation brought material great distances into Carrick but it also carried rocks out of the region. Ailsa Craig granite can be found in northern England, Isle of Man and to the southern part of the Irish Sea.

While the town of Girvan signs itself as *"Gateway to Ailsa Craig"*, the island, known locally as *The Craig*, could be considered the gateway to Carrick for it has been the magnet that has drawn many visitors to the region. So, in looking at this fascinating place, we can have an introduction to the other key elements that gives Carrick its character – history, flora and fauna.

One of the earliest travellers who recorded his impressions of Ailsa was Donald Munro, Dean of the Isles in the middle of the 16th century. The great humanist and scholar of European stature, George Buchanan, also a pensioner of Crossraguel Abbey, drew upon Donald Munro's work for his *Rerum Scoticarum Historia* published in Latin at Edinburgh in 1582.

A more famous writer, naturalist, Màrtainn MacGille Mhàrtainn (better known as Martin Martin), gives us a remarkable account in his book, *A Description of the Western Isles of Scotland* published in 1703.

"Ailsa is a big rock, about six leagues to the south-west of Arran; it rises in form of a sugar-loaf, but the top is plain, and large enough for drawing up a thousand men in ranks; there is a fresh-water lake in the middle of the plain, the whole isle is covered with long grass, and is inaccessible, except on the south-west side, by a stair cut out in the rock; in the middle of it there is a small tower of three stories high with the top. There is a fresh water spring issuing out of the side of this great rock; below the entry there is a place where the fishers take up their residence during their stay about this rock in quest of cod and ling; and there is a good anchorage for their vessels very near their tents.

This rock in the summer-time abounds with variety of sea-fowl, that build and hatch in it. The solan geese [gannets] and coulterneb [puffins] are most numerous here; the latter are by the fishers called *albanich*, which in the ancient Irish language signifies Scotsmen.

The isle has a chapel on the top called Fiunnay, and an ancient pavement or causeway. Ailsa is the Earl of Cassillis' property, the tenant who farms it pays him one hundred marks Scots yearly; the product of the isle is hogs, fowl, down, and fish."

There are several astonishing things here. Not least that the fishermen called the puffins '*Scotsmen*'. More importantly, there is evidence of a chapel at the top of the island. This could be a significant trace of early Christianity and surely demands archaeological investigation.

The writings of one naturalist stimulated another and in 1772 Thomas Pennant (1726-1798), an English-speaking Welshman from Flintshire, followed in the footsteps of Gaelic-speaking Martin Martin (1665-1718). Pennant arrived on a gentle day in June and relates the principal features of geology, flora and fauna which others do, but includes detail not found elsewhere and that is groves of elder trees and three types of snail. Surprisingly for a naturalist he considered the island, with its multitude of cacophonous birds, a place of horror but was charmed by the song birds when he wrote, "*... and what is wonderful, throstles* [thrushes] *exerted the same melody as they do in the groves of Hertfordshire*".

About 40 years after Pennant's slightly ascerbic account, the eminent surgeon and geologist, Dr John Mcculloch (1773-1835) gave valuable information on the rock structures after his visit to Ailsa.

The hazards that faced visitors to the island can be appreciated through the personal reminiscences of Revd David Landsborough (1799-1854), Presbyterian minister of Stevenston, Ayrshire. He made an excursion to Ailsa in the 1830s on a steamer from Ardrossan via Arran, with men, women and children aboard including his two sons, aged 10 and 12 years. Arduous though the trip was, both on the island and in the Firth of Clyde, it paled into insignificance for one of the boys who went on to greater adventure as an adult in Australia.

Setting out at 8 am on a pleasant day, the passengers looked forward to an hour on Ailsa. On arrival, about 15 people decided to climb to the summit while Landsborough chose to go as far as the ruined tower-house. Although the path was difficult and strewn with gigantic nettles, he still noted the campion and catchfly. Others told him of finding *Helosciadium inundatum* (a kind of marshwort) at higher levels. He had hoped, but failed, to find *Lavatera arborea* (tree mallow) which he believed grew there. The luxuriant vegetation which other writers have remarked upon was ascribed by Landsborough to the constant moist conditions and nutrient-rich guano from tens of thousands of seabirds. Drainage on steep slopes would have maintained a balance of fertiliser.

On returning to the steamer he was confronted by an anxious commotion as he and his fellow passengers realised his two young sons, who had been distracted by observing the puffins and enjoying the spectacular views from the summit, were now panicking in case the boat left without them. As the boys raced down the steep slope towards a precipitous cliff, concern turned to horror as tragedy seemed inevitable. Fortunately the nimble-footed lads stopped just in time. In later years they both emigrated to Australia where one of them, William, became a famous explorer and was the first European to cross that continent from north to south.

Another unsettling incident happened as the vessel departed the island. One of the passengers, a preacher with a musket, decided to shoot at the flocks of birds. In the 20th century it was the habit of ships' captains to sound their horns as they passed the cliffs, causing thousands of birds to take flight to the perverse delight of their passengers and crew. When it was eventually realised that the shock killed many birds, the practice was stopped.

For Landsborough's party the troubles were just about to begin. The ship ran aground. No amount of steam power could shift it and the exasperated captain ordered the passengers to gather in a group and repeatedly run from bow to stern. Still it did not budge. They had no option but to await the incoming tide which seemed ponderously slow, casting a sullen mood over the group. The boat was eventually freed but worse was to come. The weather turned very wet and windy making the return voyage to Arran uncomfortable and slow. The angry storm prevented a landing so the steamer continued to Ardrossan where a relieved Landsborough and his sons set ashore. The three-mile walk in the dark back to the manse in Stevenston was tame by comparison.

Seabird city, former residents and occasional visitors

Ailsa Craig has the third-largest gannet colony in the United Kingdom, with over 36,000 pairs. It is a Site of Special Scientific Interest, a European Special Protection Area and a nature reserve in the care of the Royal Society for the Protection of Birds under a management agreement with the Marquis of Ailsa. In the 1990s the RSPB finally eradicated rats, which first arrived during the construction of the lighthouse a hundred years earlier. This allowed the colony of puffins to be re-established. Other important populations are guillemots, kittiwakes and razorbills. Grey seals can often be seen on the rocks around the Craig and at certain times of year, harbour porpoises, basking sharks and occasional large minke whales make an appearance. As Martin Martin recorded, hogs were a product of the island. It is hard to imagine that they had enough ground to be raised economically. Wild goats bred on the island and such were their numbers that they troubled the domestic goats introduced by the Girvan family to provide milk for day-trippers. The Girvans' goats were in pens known as *goat rees*

Coulterneb:
The name comes from the blade or sharp-edged disc that cuts through the soil vertically ahead of the ploughshare. Why did 17th century fishermen on Ailsa call them *Scotsmen*?

18

but the interference from the feral animals resulted in the wild beasts becoming targets for shooting. The goat population varied between about 20 in 1902 to about 80 in 1936. By this time it was still common practice to catch puffins and salt them down for winter meat.

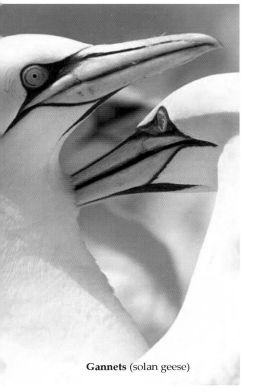

Gannets (solan geese)

Charles Kirk, Pioneering Photographer

The photographer, taxidermist and naturalist Charles Kirk (1872-1922) was born in Edinburgh, the second son of a grocer and wine merchant. The family moved to London where Charles continued his education and later chose a career apprenticed to one of Europe's leading taxidermists, Roland Ward. In 1896 Kirk set up his own taxidermy business in Glasgow, gaining a high reputation for his innovative style of presentation. This led in 1901 to a commission for the Glasgow International Exhibition and Kirk's work, *Seabirds nesting on Ailsa Craig* was based on his photography on the island.

Charles Kirk perched on Ailsa's cliffs with a stereoscopic camera to create a 3-D effect. The photograph was taken around 1900.

The scale of the cliffs can be seen by the size of the castle and the small boat in the lower picture.

The Victorian passion for stuffed birds and animals resulted in massive slaughter and Kirk, a man of his time, was part of that. He also traded in birds' eggs and skins. His photographs, which helped him create realistic backgrounds for his taxidermy specimens, were published in picture-book form. This led to an increased interest in seeing live birds rather than inanimate ones in glass cases. Charles Kirk did not restrict himself to photographing birds on the Craig. Fortunately for posterity, he recorded many other scenes from his visits there between 1896 and 1922.

Nathaniel Peabody Rogers (1894-1846)

Thanks to his work, today's naturalists can peer into the past and see the birds and the goats, while geologists and curling enthusiasts have an invaluable record of the curling stone industry. Social and family historians also have a cornucopia of images from a world that has vanished. In cultural terms, the *Kirk on the Craig* archive is of monumental proportion and deserves greater public attention.

The Abolitionist and the Actress

In 1841, American slavery abolitionist Nathaniel Peabody Rogers was captivated by the Craig even from a distance of over 20 miles. He was *en route* to Ireland with a group of Scottish abolitionists. In his newspaper column for the *Herald of Freedom*, he remorsefully reported on the captain firing a gun to cause thousands of birds to take flight in massive swirling clouds which Rogers compared, as a natural spectacle, with the Niagara Falls.

During a theatrical engagement in Glasgow in 1883, Ellen Terry, the famous Shakespearian actress, was invited by a Clyde shipyard owner, Sir William Pearce, to join him on a sail aboard his luxury yacht, *Lady Torfrida*. Accompanying them were impresario Henry Irving and his tour manager, Bram Stoker (of *Dracula* fame) as well as Ellen Terry's son and daughter by the architect Edwin Goodwin. The island cast its spell on the children who both adopted the name Craig;

Ellen Terry (1847-1928)

Edward changed his by deed poll and Edith used Ailsa Craig as her stage name for a time around 1895.

Golfers and Curlers

With television coverage of Open Golf Championships at Turnberry, one of the world's leading golf courses, the majestic backdrop of Ailsa Craig has become instantly recognisable. The popularity of curling as a winter Olympics sport has increased knowledge of, and affection for, its granite curling stones. Quarrying is no longer carried out. Only loose boulders scattered across the foreshore may be removed from the island for manufacture in Mauchline, Ayrshire.

The Lighthouse

The only inland parish in Scotland with a lighthouse is Dailly. This is as a result of Ailsa Craig being in the Marquis of Ailsa's barony of Knockgarron.
But that historical quirk aside, the lighthouse is notable for having been designed by the famous Stevenson family.

Petitions received by the Commissioners of Northern Lighthouses in 1881 from Lloyds and the Scottish Shipmasters Association requested two fog signals and a lighthouse on Ailsa Craig. Work began the following year and an oil-burning light was first exhibited on the night of 15th June, 1886, seven years before its sister light was established at Turnberry. The construction of both was supervised by Thomas and David Stevenson, engineers to the Northern Lighthouses Board. Thomas was the father of Robert Louis Stevenson.

Mr Girvan

Astonishingly, the light keepers and employees of Ailsa Craig Granites Ltd depended upon carrier pigeons for communication with the mainland until 1935 when wireless telephone communications were established. A pigeon house was built at Girvan Green, and pigeons were provided by the lighthouse boatman at that time, who received an annual payment of £4. If a doctor or supplies were urgently needed and stormy weather prevented the use of the pigeons, a system of signals by fire was used.

5 COAST

"Now the summer's in prime
Wi' the flowers richly blooming,
And the wild mountain thyme
A' the moorlands perfuming."

Robert Tannahill, (1774 – 1810), Paisley poet
and founder of a Burns Club there in 1803

Wild thyme (*Thymus praecox*) can be found in pockets of base-rich turf on Bennane Hill.

As with many aspects of Scotland, the key word is diversity. The flora and fauna of Carrick have a considerable variety of habitats, from the exposed, salt-blasted coast and windswept hills to sheltered glens and formal country-house policies. It is no surprise that around two-thirds of Ayrshire's Sites of Special Scientific Interest (SSSIs) are in the region.

Scotland's extreme oceanic climate is unique in Europe and is characterised by cool summers and mild winters. However, there are no extreme conditions such as drought, tornadoes or earthquakes. The Gulf Stream, or North Atlantic Drift, warms the Firth of Clyde and its benign influence can be seen in palm trees that have become popular in local gardens. The prevailing winds from the south-west carry salt quite far inland. In addition the combination of plants drawing water from a salty substrate, frequent winds and high sunlight, cause their rates of water loss to be high. However, adaptation to habitat has taken place over many generations.

Beaches and Cliffs

Ayrshire has a large number of sand, shingle and pebble beaches. At Turnberry, where the dunes provide the perfect setting for links golf courses, the calcareous shell sand encourages wildflower species such as lady's fingers, yellow rattle, restharrow and several varieties of orchids. At first glance it may appear as if nature has been banished by carefully manicured fairways and greens. But the "roughs" and "out-of-bounds" areas of the golf courses remain virtually untouched, allowing plants and wildlife to survive unhindered.

Rocky shores, sea cliffs and salt marshes show a zoning of plants within comparatively short distances. The most salt-resistant vegetation exists at the bottom of cliffs and the edges of marshes nearest the sea. In the places within the sea-spray zone can be found varieties of black, yellow and grey lichens. Above that, salt-resistant species of plantain and milkwort can grow in crevices. At the Heads of Ayr the salt-resistant halophytes are accompanied by primrose, wild hyacinth and red campion in sheltered areas, while in exposed parts thrift, sea campion, bird's foot trefoil and scentless mayweed grow alongside heaths, blackthorn and bramble.

Good examples of rocky shoreline plants can also be found along the coast at Dunure and Culzean, where the nationally scarce southern polypody (*Polypodium cambricum*) and local rarities such as rock samphire (*Crithmum maritimum*) and wood vetch (*Vicia sylvatica*) can be found. Further south, the shingle beach at Ballantrae is noted for its wide range of coastal plants including a large colony of the rare oyster plant, *Mertensia maritima*.

At Culzean, between Barwhin Point and Swallow Craigs, is the best coastal deciduous woodland in southern Scotland. Ash, sycamore, wych-elm and aspen provide a canopy for well developed ground flora including dog's mercury (*Mercurialis perennis*), opposite-leaved golden saxifrage (*Chrysosplenium oppositifolium*) and locally uncommon hart's tongue (*Phyllitis scolopendrium*). Similar woodland is found at the north of this SSSI by the Carwinshoch Burn where there is extensive scrubland comprising blackthorn, hawthorn and whin. Bennane Head Grasslands SSSI 3 miles south of Lendalfoot, is a rare example of lowland neutral grassland in Scotland. It supports a diverse range of flowering plants which includes the only Scottish population of green-winged orchids (*Orchis morio*). The dominant species of grass include sheep's fescue (*Festuca ovina*), sweet vernal-grass (*Anthoxanthum odoratum*) and crested dog's tail (*Cynosurus cristatus*). A number of herbs such as eyebright (*Euphrasia officinalis*) and selfheal (*Prunella vulgaris*) are also present. Small, rocky knolls provide pockets of support for saxifrages and clovers.

6 WETLANDS

**Common
spotted orchid**

*"We think na on the lang Scots miles,
The mosses, waters, slaps and stiles"*

Robert Burns (1759-1796): *Tam o Shanter*

Place-names are an excellent way to "read" the countryside. Learning the basic terms is less arduous for ramblers than unexpectedly having to clamber over ridges or skirt wetlands. Before the great farm drainage schemes in the 18th century, large tracts of land were lost to bog and marsh. This is reflected in the place-names such as *moss* which is the Scots word for marsh or the Gaelic *moine séanta* (Minishant, *holy moss,* which is next to Monkwood) or *dubh pol* (Dipple, *dark pool*).

While some features such as ditches can be fairly modern, acid peat bogs reach back thousands of years to the end of the last Ice Age. The retreating glaciers and melting ice created hundreds of lochs and lochans. The shallower ones were colonised by various sphagnum mosses which sometimes could blanket the loch surface.

Feoch Meadows SSSI, near Barrhill, has one of the finest grasslands in Ayrshire. Along the Feoch Burn are neutral grasslands interspersed with low-lying marshy areas which support plants rare in the county such as spignel (*Meum athamanticum*), whorled caraway (*Carum verticillatum*) field gentian (*Gentianella campestris*) and several varieties of orchid. The deeper pools in the burn provide habitats for yellow water lily while the small gorges contain locally-scarce globeflower (*Trollius europaeus*) and willow (*Salix repens*). At Knockdaw Hill, to the east of Lendalfoot, purple moor grass (*Molina caerula*) can be found where ground water reaches the surface. Nearby, at Craig Hill, there is a varied sequence of mire types with species-rich communities.

Riverbanks

The rich mix of (sometimes intermingling) languages in the region gives us great variety and a fair degree of accuracy in describing watercourses. Lack of understanding by incomers of an indigenous language, though, has led to tautology such as Albany Burn, outside Barr, which appears in a 17ᵗʰ century map as *Alten Albenach Burn*, that is, the *Scotsmen's stream burn* (from the Gaelic *allt*, a stream). Double naming is often commonly found with hills; Knockdaw Hill is an example where the *Knock* element is from the Gaelic *cnoc*, small hill.

Larger than a burn are watercourses such as Water of App, Water of Tig and Water of Assel which are small in comparison with a major river, Water of Girvan. At the top of the tree, or more correctly, bottom of the valley, is the majestic River Doon which defines the northern and eastern boundaries of Carrick. It is an ancient name of obscure origin, possibly pre-Celtic. Place-names of course may no longer give clues as they originated hundreds of years ago and landscapes change. But there will always be quirks such as the wee loch, Lake Superior in Galloway, just over Carrick's south-western border.

Rivers and streams, while providing distinctive habitats also act as transporters of seeds, which in recent times have brought the spread of the unwelcome, non-native giant hogweed. Flood plains and flush areas create a succession of habitats on fens and mires where alder, willow and downy birch are the predominant species. Native woodlands can be seen in the oak and birch along the Penwhapple Burn (an important geological site) and the Doon between Dalrymple and Smithston, while Glen Tig is noted for mixed ash.

The Craig Wood SSSI near Heronsford in this glen, has mixed ash, elm and oak woodland on the riverside flats and lower valley slopes. Loch Lochton, on the eastern side of Grey Hill, is a rare example of a natural body of water on serpentinite. It is home to various water lilies and sedges including the only known Scottish location for a particular hybrid *Carex x beckmanii*.

Landscapes are constantly, albeit imperceptibly, changing. Abstraction of water for modern farming can lower the water table and alter long-established habitants. If climate change predictions are correct and Scotland experiences warmer and wetter weather in future then that too will alter the landscape. One thing is certain: flora and fauna will adjust to all changes.

FLORA

River Stinchar: made famous by Robert Burns in his poem, *My Nanie, O* with the words, *"Behind yon hills where Stinchar flows, 'Mang moors an' mosses many, O"*.

Orchids at Garnaburn, between Craig Hill and Clauchanton Hill, Colmonell © Harriet Ellis

7 GRASSLANDS, WOODS & ESTATES

*"Jock, when ye hae naething else to do, ye may be aye sticking in a tree;
it will be growing, Jock, when yer sleeping."*

Sir Walter Scott (1771-1832): *Heart of Midlothian*

Common rockrose

Scotland has always had a low density of population. Therefore, the need to work difficult soils had never been pressing. However, agrarian reform in the late 17th and early 18th centuries led to extensive land drainage schemes and the introduction of larger herds of cattle and flocks of sheep. Later developments with modern fertilisers continued and accelerated the rate of change with the consequential loss of wildflower meadows and that most delightful of song birds, the skylark. Add to that the grubbing out of hedgerows and, to many eyes, we are left with a green desert. Fortunately, landowners and farmers now take a more enlightened attitude with increasing interest in organic farming and the creation of wildlife corridors.

Natural grasslands have now largely been restricted to protected sites, with which Carrick is well endowed. The Lendalfoot Hills Complex, classified as a Special Area of Conservation, extends to over 1,300 hectares (3,212 acres) and has within its feature habitats, grasslands on soils rich with heavy metals and species-rich grassland in upland areas. Similarly at Knockdolian, 3 km (2 miles) north of Ballantrae, the diversity of grassland species reflects the rarity of the underlying geology. At a much lower altitude is Auchalton, south of Crosshill, where

Killochan (private)

there are areas of dry and wet grassland on the site of a former limeworks with species-rich plant communities including orchids. Spanning the gap between the lowland grasslands of Auchalton and the uplands around Ballantrae and is Feoch Meadows to the east of Barrhill where the complex of grassland types covers upland as well as the lowland/upland fringe.

Woods

As with other aspects of the landscape, place-names tell us that the bare hills were not always so. Elements from Gaelic and Scots such as *beoch* (birch), *darroch* (oak) and *sauch* (willow) give us clues to the past. The tranquillity of modern-day woodland is in stark contrast to medieval times when they had an important economic role. They provided fuel as well as raw materials for building, tanning, charcoal-burning and the manufacture of farm implements. In addition they gave shelter to deer and boar which provided meat and many by-products. As the population grew over the centuries, the woods declined to such an extent that it was commonly remarked upon by travellers.

The two 16th century maps of Carrick by Timothy Pont show tree cover mostly confined to the country houses and the southern river valleys of the Doon, Girvan and Stinchar. Over 200 years later Armstrong's map indicates little had changed but he, unlike Pont, includes numerous areas of rough pasture or marsh. Some written records indicate tracts of natural forest in Ayrshire and a charter of Crossraguel Abbey to Sir William Kennedy of Brunston in 1569 refers to the annual cutting of timber known in Scots as *woodhag*.

Designed Landscapes

Cassillis House (*private*) in late 18th century

"There is no way under the sun so probable for improving our land as inclosing and planting the same: therefore I wish it were effectually put into practice."

The sentiments of John Reid concluding his book, *The Scots Gard'ner* in 1683 were put into practice by the owners of large country houses. A contemporary writer, Revd William Abercrombie, of Maybole, described numerous country seats as being *"well wooded"*. He singled out Dalquharran with its great woods and mighty oaks as *"the best house of all that country"*.

Opposite: 1775 map by Capt. Armstrong

Camp Hill

Mains Wallaceton Drumquean

Dinnimacks Drumshean Burntstone ruins Dalquharran Balbeg Maitland

Sned Blair Blair Lime Poundla

Blair Craig Lime Kilns Manse Roan Muirstoun Langside Merkland

Woodhead Bargeny Daily Smithston

Woodside Sandbed Drongan Park Mauchrikill Knockrocker ruins

Kilochan Girvan Belcamy Kilkerran ruins

Caraw Cnig Lindsaystoun Drumbain

Boyds Hall Lovestoun Gallenston Dumlamfort

Dalvehir Brakenbrae Hadvad Pinblaith

Old Daily Hawkhill Glengenet

Killoup ruins Corfin

Brae Cannagan Pinkill ruins Bilgarry Miljoan Milton Stin

Luiten Glengenet

Beldetchie Pengerroch Glengenet Barr

Fomichael C A R R Mill

Auchenwooch Barr

Drumern Letterpin Delfask Auchenseule Albany Barr Shang

As Hills Kirkdominie Dalgarvan

Kirklands ruins Dowlar Dinmurchie Gregg

Holms Lochstone

Kilpatrick Cairn

Balloch Terbock

Pendlan Lambdoughty Merk Darlae

Pinmore

At the Nick of Darlae & half a Mile West,
the Road leads on the Side of a very steep
Hill, its not above two feet broad and if you
stumble you must fall almost Perpendicular
six or seven Hundred Feet.

L. Shalloch

Daljerick Doughramiel Kilbride

Muck R. Cawan

Ballimore Garlathan

Hallow Chapel Lump G. Shilloch Halfmark Tyfoil

Farden Span Well
Much frequented
in Summer

Penwhir Conachy

ruins Barby Loch

A number of these major improvements with walled gardens, orchards and parks have survived into modern times. But others, mainly smaller estates, have been lost in places like Baltersan, Knockdaw Castle, Benan in the Stinchar valley and three along the Muck Water – Fardenreoch, Docherniel and Bellamore.

Although Scots pine and native broadleaf species formed the bulk of the planting on smaller estates, the bigger landowners competed for status with exotic trees, encouraged by the 19th century plant collectors who scoured the globe for specimens that would flourish in Scotland's temperate climate. Significant plantations were established at Craigengillen near Loch Doon and to the south-east of Girvan at Balkeachy and Tormitchell. One import popular with country gardens that is no longer welcome is *Rhododendron ponticum*. When it is in flower in places like the beautiful gardens of Bargany it is a magnificent sight but its brief blossoming spectacle is at a terrible cost to native flora and fauna. Considerable efforts are now being made throughout the United Kingdom to eradicate it.

In contrast to the formal walks, stately avenues and "rustic" woodlands of the country houses is the natural woodland protected in sites such as Craig Wood, Knockdolian, Glen App and in places between Maidens and Doonfoot. Unlike the dreaded rhododendron which stifles everything beside and beneath it, these woodlands give shelter to a profusion of native flora and fauna that makes walking in Carrick such a rewarding experience. For it is amongst the oak and the birch that one may find species such as hard fern (*Blechnum spicant*), broad buckler fern (*Dryopteris dilatata*), juniper and orchids. Beneath the mixed ash woodlands are alternate-leaved golden saxifrage (*Chrysosplenium alternifolium*), Wilson's filmy fern (*Hymenophyllum wilsonii*), toothwort (*Lathraea squamaria*), herb Paris (*Paris quadrifolia*) and aspen (*Populus tremula*).

Bargany (private): a fine late-17th c. house set in beautiful policies; its predecessor was described by Timothy Pont as, "*A huge, great, lofty tower in the centre of a quadrangular court that had on each of three corners fine well built towers of freestone, four storeys high.*"

8   UPLANDS

"Pluck not the wayside flower;,
It is the traveller's bower.

William Allingham (1824-1889), Irish poet

North Carrick

The diversity of habitats that is such a feature of Carrick can be experienced by a walk from the shore at Dunure to the top of Brown Carrick Hill where the highest point is 287 metres (942 feet) above sea level. From the summit there is a magnificent panorama of the Firth of Clyde and the town of Ayr. For the naturalist, there is an astonishing variety of flora and fauna within a distance of 3 kilometres or just under two miles.

Spring sandwort
(*Minuartia verna*)

Starting at sea level, basalt rocks are home to lichens, seaweeds, thrift and rare saltwort. Above the beach of sand, gravel and pebbles can be found bladderwort, yellow iris, sand spurrey, sea sandwort, sea purslane and marram grass. There is then terracing of three levels of ancient raised beach where dry areas at the top of the middle cliffs are colonised by heathers, bramble, blackthorn, whin (gorse), harebell, and bird's foot trefoil. The sand and pebble loam at this level supports milkwort, eyebright, rock-rose and vernal squill.

Dunure Station:
early 20th c.
and early 21st c.

The upper raised beach at around 45 metres above the shore has a similar soil but includes clay washed down from glacial till. The damp areas at the base of these former shoreline cliffs provide a habitat for flag iris, globe flower, primrose and meadowsweet. Beneath the trees above this cliff are wood anemone, garlic, bluebells, dog's mercury and wood avens. A short distance uphill the disused railway cutting and stream valleys provide undisturbed locations for hawthorn, sycamore, willow, alder, bramble, hemp agrimony (which is very attractive to bees and butterflies), elderberry and blackthorn (sloe).

Next there is an extensive area of improved pasture and arable land with rocky outcrops including a glacial crag and tail feature at the 120 metre contour at Dunduff. Beyond this is an area of improved grazing up to its limit at the 170 metre contour. The final vertical ascent of about 70-100 metres has conifer plantations at the lower end with hill grazing and rough pasture where damp hollows contain butterwort, orchid, lousewort, rare grass-of-parnassus, bogbean, sphagnum mosses and ferns. In the drier areas are blaeberry, whin, broom, eyebright, potentilla, heath and heathers.

South Carrick

Here are the most interesting upland habitats in the region where flora overlies volcanic rocks and glaciation has gouged out valleys and rounded hills. Knockdolian, known as the "false Craig" for its reputation of deceiving sailors on watch for Ailsa Craig, is unusual for the extent of its subalpine calcareous grassland to be found at such low altitude. The conical peak only reaches 265 metres. The composition of the diverse species reflects the underlying serpentinite and other ultra-basic rocks of the Ballantrae Complex. The same conditions apply at nearby Littleton and Balhamie Hills, 2 km south of Lendalfoot. On the better drained soils here, especially on the south-facing slopes, there is a great variety of species including fescue and bents with common milkwort, mouse-ear hawkweed, lady's bedstraw and northern bedstraw. Flushed areas have common centaury and bog pimpernel.

Further examples of species-rich areas can be found on the neighbouring line of hills of Knockornal, Knockdaw and Aldons. An area with similar characteristics is the Pinbain Burn to Cairnhill SSSI to the south of Girvan. It is biologically important as it is one of the few sites in the country where uninterrupted topographical sequences of vegetation can be seen. Part of this site is dominated by Grey Hill and Fell Hill which look down on Kennedy's Pass on the coast road. On a plateau to the east, a distinctive mire community has developed with a variety of sedges and other bog-tolerant plants. The dry acid grassland of the granite slopes on Grey Hill is home to fescues, bents and wavy-hair grass. The south-facing slopes have fine, species-rich grasslands with the colourful plants, thyme, common rock-rose and kidney vetch. Where the underlying serpentinite is near or on the surface there are occurrences of the locally uncommon juniper and nationally scarce spring sandwort and alpine pennycress. As elsewhere in Carrick, the ascent of these hills is richly rewarded, not only by the wide variety of flora but by the magnificent views from the summits.

9 RIVERS, COAST & SEA

"Qua sa ever be convict of slauchter of Salmonde, in time forbidden by the Lawe, he sall pay fourtie schillinges for the unlaw. And at the third time, gif he be convict of sik trespasse, he sall tyne his life, or then bye it. And gif onie man be infeft to fish in forbidden time, all sik priviledges sall cease for thrie zeiris to-cum. And gif onie dois the contrair, he sall tine ane hundredth shillings for the unlaw before the Justice."

Act of Parliament, 1424 decreeing the death penalty for a third offence of taking salmon out of season.

Otter

almon have an ancient lineage in Scotland. They appear on Dark Age Pictish stones, Crossraguel Abbey had salmon fishing rights on the Water of Girvan and Ayr Burgh controlled salmon fishing by net and coble boat on the River Doon in the 16th century. Although considered a luxury in modern times, it became a cause of complaint for estate workers in the 18th and 19th centuries when their wages were paid too often in salmon.

The Doon, Girvan and Stinchar rivers are still fished for salmon but by recreational anglers. The once species-rich Firth of Clyde has had a sudden and dramatic change in the 20th century with considerable reductions in round and flat fish. This probably accounts for the increase in scallops and *Nephrops norvegicus*, a crustacean better known as "scampi", which forms the mainstay of commercial fishing in the firth today. Others harvested, but to a much lesser degree, are lobster, crab and mussels.

The last commercial net fishing along the Carrick coast ended at the mouth of the River Doon in 1996. It had been managed by the Carson family for 46 years until 1984. With the net and coble catches peaking at 8,700 salmon and grilse in the 1960s, it was Ayrshire's most productive fishery since the collapse of the herring industry at Ballantrae.

Recreational angling

Recreational angling is an important element of the rural economy. Each of Carrick's three main rivers offers its own distinctive qualities to the game fisher. Salmon fishing on the majestic Doon comes into its own in late summer and peaks in October. It is supplied by the expansive Loch Doon which is useful in times of drought. The Water of Girvan and the picturesque Stinchar are small spate rivers where salmon, grilse and sea trout can be caught.

Other fish species

Pike, perch and grayling are well known to anglers in the region but the most interesting is the Arctic charr (*Salvelinus alpinus*) in Loch Doon. This species used to migrate to the sea but became isolated when temperatures rose after the last Ice Age. It is the reason for the loch's designation as a Site of Special Scientific Interest. Not quite so important but still of interest are the three-spine stickleback (*Gasterosteus aculeatus*) and stone loach (*Nemacheilus barbatus*). The latter is considered to be a non-native species, having been introduced as live bait.

River Stinchar at Colmonell

Lampreys (brook, river and sea) are widely distributed although the river and sea species migrate to the sea as adults. Being unable to pass obstacles which the faster and strong salmon and trout can overcome means lampreys are not found in the upper reaches of Carrick's rivers. They are extremely reclusive, hiding all their juvenile life in burrows within silt beds. The best time to catch a glimpse of them is during the breeding season, which is March to April for the brook and river species. Although as adults they are normally nocturnal, migrating at night, they often spawn in open areas of river in daytime making themselves vulnerable to predators.

Eels (*Anguilla anguilla*) are also widespread but there is European concern for population numbers so, as a conservation measure, legislation prohibits fishing by any method for eels in Scotland unless under a special licence.

Otters

Eels, salmon and trout form a main part of the otter's diet. Otters are also known to feed on crabs, frogs and, to a lesser extent, small mammals and some birds. The species was in serious decline in the second half of the 20th century but that situation has been reversed due to the phasing out of some hydrocarbon pesticides. The Scottish population is one of the largest in Europe, making it of global importance. It is protected by Scottish, UK and European legislation. Otters live close to rivers, lochs and marshes. Those that live beside the sea maintain the waterproof quality of their fur by regularly washing in fresh water. Keen-eyed observers have spotted otters in several Carrick locations, including the waters of Girvan harbour.

Seals

These charming, gregarious creatures with soulful eyes can be seen basking on rocks in various places along the coast, on Ailsa Craig or swimming near to shore. Seals are friendly and curious mammals, often swimming close to vessels in an enquiring fashion. The two species found around Scotland are the grey seal (*Halichoerus grypus*) - the dominant species in the Firth of Clyde - and the common (or harbour) seal (*Phoca vitulina*). The Scottish populations of each represent about 90% of the UK total.

Basking Sharks and Cetaceans

The distinctive black fin of the fearsome-looking but docile basking shark has become a common sight in the Firth of Clyde. In recent years it has been accompanied by several cetaceans including minke whales, porpoise and bottlenose dolphin. As the gateway to the ocean, the stretch of sea off the Carrick coast may provide a glimpse of very rare visitors such as the humpback whale.

Sea creatures are rarely seen but they form a vital component in the world's biodiversity. Their sustainable conservation is now taken seriously so that the mistakes of the past are not repeated. In the 1880s an astonishing 500,000 people in Scotland were involved, one way and another, in the fishing industry. All that has changed, but the need for concerted conservation measures that take account of nature and the country's economy is recognised by the national parliament.

10 MOTHS & BUTTERFLIES

"The fluttering of a butterfly's wing can affect climate changes on the other side of the planet."

Paul Erlich (b. 1932), American entomologist

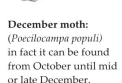

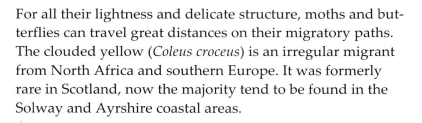

December moth: (*Poecilocampa populi*) in fact it can be found from October until mid or late December.

T he most species-rich fauna in Scotland is easily the invertebrates. Insects alone account for about 14,000 species. Limitations of space means it would be wise to focus on a group that's most easily observed, the highly-attractive Lepidoptera (butterflies and moths).

Butterflies

Bird's foot trefoil is sought out by the dingy skipper butterfly to lay its eggs.

For all their lightness and delicate structure, moths and butterflies can travel great distances on their migratory paths. The clouded yellow (*Coleus croceus*) is an irregular migrant from North Africa and southern Europe. It was formerly rare in Scotland, now the majority tend to be found in the Solway and Ayrshire coastal areas.

Thirty-four species of butterflies are now resident or regular visitors to west and south-west Scotland. Distributions of many of them have been changing, often dramatically in recent years, almost certainly as a result of climate change. There have been major expansions in the range of four butterflies and others have shown more gradual increases. Two species have recently been recorded in Scotland for the first time for over a hundred years and another one has been recorded in Scotland for the first time ever.

The dingy skipper (*Erynnis tages*) is probably now Scotland's most endangered butterfly. It has two widely separated populations – one in Dumfries and Galloway and Ayrshire and the other in north-east Scotland, mainly along the Moray Firth. It has disappeared from several sites in recent years. However, it seems to be able to survive at very low population levels and go undetected for several years. It was unrecorded at Pinbain Burn, near Lendalfoot, a frequently visited site on the Ayrshire coast between 1997 and 2006, but was rediscovered there in 2007 and was seen again in 2008.

Pinbain Burn, Hill and quarry all feature frequently in the record of earliest and latest sightings of butterflies in the west of Scotland with appearances by large skipper (*Ochlodes sylvanus*), northern brown argus (*Plebeius artaxerxes*), grayling (*Hipparchia semele*), small copper (*Lycaena phlaeas*) and the rare dingy skipper. Commonly we think of butterflies as big and colourful, and moths as small and dismal. But the dingy skipper's wingspan is only 27-34 mm, and the drab colouring of grey and brown wavy-patterns on its wings is a camouflage well adapted to its habitat. Males emerge from May to June and set about protecting their territory and finding a mate. Females seek out the common plant, bird's foot trefoil (*Lotus coniculatus*) on which to lay their round, greenish-white eggs. This plant can be found at Heads of Ayr, the raised beach of Dunure, Bennane Head grassland and on the south-facing slopes of Pinbain Hill.

Pearl-bordered fritillary (*Boloria euphrosyne*) is still widespread in the west of Scotland and the Highlands. However, several colonies in the south-west have been lost in the last 30 years It is, like the grayling, a priority species in the UK Biodiversity Action Plan, along with small pearl-bordered fritillary (*Boloria selene*), the northern brown argus and wall brown (*Lasiommata megera*) which have been found in Glen App, Lendalfoot and at Pinbain.

Recent arrivals in Scotland from England are the Essex skipper and small skipper, which have similar colouring to the large skipper. The only confirmed sighting of the Essex skipper has been in Birkshaw Forest near Lockerbie in Dumfries-shire, but the large skipper is established in Carrick, appearing in the list of earliest and latest sightings of its species in the season, at Lendalfoot.

Grayling, one of 11 priority species in the west and south-west of Scotland identified in the UK BAP, breeds on the dry coastal grasslands at Culzean. Land management here, such as the thinning of tree cover to create glades, has encouraged ground flora and butterflies while maintaining the landscape value of the woodland.

Dark green fritillary
© Fred Westcott

Left:
Six-spot burnet

Below:
Merveille du jour

Pictures courtesy
of Neil Gregory,
County Moth
Recorder

Orange tip
© Fred Westcott

Moths

Of the 432 species of moth recorded in Carrick, Culzean Country Park can boast a staggering 341 including square-spotted clay (*Xestia rhomboidea*), a priority species in the UK BAP along with 11 other species found in Scotland. There are over 2,400 species of moth recorded in the British Isles, so it is no surprise that knowledge of the status of the various populations is very limited. Apart from the scale of the required study, there is perhaps an image problem for this creature which is perceived to be dull and is associated with eating clothes and flying into lampshades on summer evenings.

And yet, one glance at a sample of moths that can be found in Carrick would dispel those prejudices. For brilliance, drama and elegance it would be hard to beat these six specimens: brimstone moth (*Opisthograptis luteolata*), canary-shouldered thorn (*Ennomos alniaria*), garden tiger (*Arctia caja*), merveille du jour (*Dichonia aprilina*), six-spotted burnet (*Zygaena filipendulae*) and yellow shell (*Camptogramma bilineata*).

The views from Carrick's hills and coasts can be breathtaking and, in certain conditions, spell-binding. But strolling, rambling and hiking would be all the more enriching if the eyes were occasionally cast downward to search for these fugitive and delicate members of the region's fauna. They are masters of camouflage, and so a sighting is not just a pleasure, it is a victory.

Left: **Brimstone moth**

Below: **December moth**

Pictures courtesy of Neil Gregory,
County Moth Recorder

11 BIRDS OF COAST & COUNTRY

Barn owl

"Anent the eschewing of great trouble, discord, and divers inconvenientes that may cum, anent the stealing of Haulkes and Houndes: It is statute and ordained, that in time cumming na maner of persons takes an uther mans hounds, nor haulkes, maid or wilde, out of nestes nor eggs out of nestes within ane uther manis ground, but licence of the Lord, under the pain of ten poundes. And in likewise na egges be tane out of the Pertrickes, nor wilde-duik-nestes, under the pain of fourtie shillings."

Act of Parliament, 9th May, 1474

Carrick hawks were much sought-after for sport by the kings of Scots, especially James IV (1472-1513) who even had his portrait painted holding a falcon. Raptors such as owls, kestrels, peregrine falcons, buzzards and sparrowhawks can today be found in the region to the delight of the eagle-eyed and the dismay of lovers of small song birds. Although the seabird "city" of Ailsa Craig grabs attention by virtue of the colossal scale of breeding pairs, the whole coast of Carrick offers numerous "villages" or colonies of birds. Several hundred species may be seen through the seasons.

Cunning Park to Greenan

From the mouth of the River Doon, including the only part of Carrick north of that river at Cunning Park, to Greenan Castle a mile away near the Heads of Ayr, is a popular bird watching area with a variety of habitats. The former rabbit warren of Cunning Park is now a marshy area of rough pasture bordered on two sides by houses and on the others by a beach walkway and a busy road. Close by is the mouth of the River Doon and a small, wooded peninsula formed by the mill race of a long-gone mill. Just south of that are mussel beds, mudflats and rocks which are exposed at low tide. The whole stretch is bordered by dune grasslands, and at Greenan Castle there are cliffs and scrubland.

Gulls, wildfowl and waders are a common sight from late July to April. In autumn, over 1,000 curlews roost at night. Lapwing and golden plover can also be seen through autumn and winter. Two species of over-wintering ducks that have been in long-term decline can be seen along this part of the coast; the goldeneye and the pochard. Harsh winters in mainland Europe can cause an influx of ducks such as the pochard and tufted duck, the latter also suffering long-term decline in Scotland. Other winter visitors are glaucous and Iceland gulls from the Arctic. Catching sight of birds is, of course, only part of the story. The delight of bird song in spring and summer can be enjoyed in the grassland and scrub at Greenan Castle where whitethroats, warblers and stonechats seek out their mates. In the woodland near the mouth of the Doon, chiffchaff and blackcap can be heard. But ruling over them all at this scenic spot is the colourful kingfisher.

A short distance inland, along a stretch of the disused Ayr to Girvan coastal railway cutting, can be found many of the smaller birds which derive shelter from gardens, hedgerows, woodland and the undisturbed vegetation of the cutting. Depending on the season, finches, tits, warblers, robins, thrushes and wrens can be seen. They are accompanied by larger birds such as grey heron, mallard, goosander and pheasant.

Culzean Country Park

This magnificent estate spreads over 600 acres, half of which is mixed, mature woodland. On the seaward side are 30-metre-high cliffs, a rocky shoreline and sandy bays. Unsurprisingly it is the most popular attraction managed by the National Trust for Scotland with over 200,000 visitors a year. The fauna statistics are impressive. It is a Listed Wildlife Site and over 100 species of bird can be found there with almost half of the total using it as a breeding ground.

To the range of habitats can be added the 50 or so buildings within the estate from the spectacularly sited neo-classical castle by and the equally impressive stable block to simple cottages and the walled garden where nesting space for swallows has reached saturation point. Those other delightful summer residents, swift and house martin also proliferate. In some ways Culzean Castle and Country Park encapsulates the essence of this book because in its extent it has so much evidence of the region's volcanic origins, its history and its flora and fauna. It is very well documented elsewhere so attention can safely be transferred to other, lesser-known places of interest.

The hunter and the hunted

Barn owl

One of the most impressive countryside birds whose habitats have been in decline for nearly 50 years. Some areas such as Carrick have stabilised and show slight signs of improvement. Scotland has about 800 birds, representing 20% of the UK's estimated population.

Pheasant (male)
© Tara-Jay Porter

A common game bird; can be seen in open countryside, hedgerows and roadsides. It is, of course, hunted by humans, not barn owls.

Maidens to Turnberry

The shoreline between these two points has both rocky and dune-fringed sandy beaches which attract a variety of seabirds and waders, either over-wintering or on passage elsewhere. A wide variety of other species is present according to the time of year. Golf courses are wildlife havens and Turnberry is no exception. But respecting the fauna should be matched by a similar respect for the golfers across whose fairways visitors need to pass to reach the lighthouse, a particularly good vantage point for bird watching. The shoreline from here to Girvan is a mix of sand dunes and raised beaches with the chance of seeing many of the species found further up the coast.

Ballantrae Shingle Beach and Glen App

This is a species-rich area for bird watchers. Breeding birds include three types of tern: the common, the arctic and the nationally-important little tern. Just 8 km (5 miles) further south is another site, Glen App, which, like Ballantrae, is designated as being of special scientific interest. Its heavy scrub and open moorlands provide hunting grounds for a range of raptors.

Knockdolian

Mature oak woodland is rare in Ayrshire so the number of typical woodland breeding bird populations attracted to this SSSI is equally special. A wide variety of birds can be found along the river valley with the occasional visit by the much-cherished and extremely rare osprey.

Lapwing:
© Fred Westcott

Also known in Scots as peesweep, peeweet and peesie.

Inland Birds

Further inland around Barr is a network of over 30 km (19 miles) of pathways including four that are way-marked. The 6.5 km (4 miles) of The Devil's Trail offers the greatest diversity of habitat. Many charming small song birds are present, as are several types of raptors such as hen harrier and short-eared owl. Similar signposted pathways have been constructed around Straiton, another popular birding location, where the woodlands are home to jay, kestrel, siskin and redpoll.

The flood plain of the Water of Girvan at Dailly offers yet another group of habitats from woodland to farmland to Brunston Golf Course which is the haunt of barn owl. On a smaller scale, but no less interesting to birders, is Heart Loch, by Maybole. Its reed-fringed pools attract wetland breeders and passing migrants. Regular visitors are warblers, reed bunting and kingfisher.

At 775 metres (2,542 feet), Shalloch on Minnoch is the highest point in Ayrshire. It is known as a "Corbett" and its euphonious Gaelic name is pronounced *Shee-loch on Minn-och*, meaning the middle place of the willow. As may be expected in this wild and exposed place, the dominant species are red grouse, black grouse, golden plover and raven. There are many other species in the area but one non-flying one to look out for is the elusive adder, the country's only poisonous snake.

These are just a few of many places in Carrick where the bird watcher and the bird lover can be treated to an ever-changing parade of hundreds of species. Although some can be seen from a car, their distinctive cries and bird song cannot be heard. So the best way to enjoy Carrick's fauna is to be out in the fresh air but with this caution: wildlife should be viewed with the minimum of disturbance to the creatures themselves and to the landowners whose fields are their living. Scotland has some of the most progressive legislation for countryside access. Knowing your access rights before going into the country is just as important as knowing the Highway Code before taking to the roads.

12 BEASTS & BATS

"Two great hart antlers decorated with attractive candlesticks, fleur-de-lys long iron chains from the crown, welded with knobs, all well painted with red lead and other fine colours, priced at £ 40."

Inventory item from the Castle of Sanquhar-Hamilton, Ayr, 1559

There are 62 wild mammal species in Scotland, of which 48 breed on land. Half the total are native to Scotland; a comparatively small number due to the country's separation from continental Europe after the last Ice Age.

Red squirrel

Bat

One of the smallest mammals, and the only one which can fly, is the bat. There are eight or nine species in Scotland, three of which are identified as significant in Carrick. They are the common pipistrelle (*Pipistrellus pipistrellus*), noctule (*Nyctalus noctula*) and whiskered bat (*Myotis mystacinus*). The largest population in the region is the pipistrelle which favours woodland edges and open woodland as well as marsh and over water as its habitat. Weighing only three to eight grams it can consume 3,000 insects in a night. Brown long-eared bats (*Plecotus auritis*) are the second-most common in the area. They too favour open woodlands, both deciduous and coniferous.

Rare whiskered bats prefer to roost in buildings and can be seen in villages and parks. Its genus relative, Daubenton's bat (*Myotis daubentonii*) prefers to be in caves, mines or underneath bridges but always near water, which is one of its main feeding grounds along with woodland and flat countryside. One of the largest bats in Europe is the noctule. It can be found in open habitats, wetlands, pasture land and even large gardens.

Squirrel

It comes as a shock to learn that one of the most enchanting creatures, the red squirrel (*Sciuris vulgaris*), is a rodent, in the same class as voles, mice and rats. However, it does not usually invade human habitation and, thanks to its charming looks and manner, it is adored. Like so many of the good things in nature, it is under threat. Loss of habitat in the form of native pine woods is one reason, but that can be remedied through enlightened land management. The other cause is the spread of the grey squirrel (*Sciuris carolinensis*) which prefers deciduous woodland where it feeds on nuts, seeds, fungi, fruit and tree bark. This unwelcome intruder carries *squirrel pox*, a viral disease deadly to red squirrels. It is believed to have reached Scotland through infected grey squirrels introduced to southern England from America in the early 20th century.

Both species are found across Carrick but the red squirrel population is thinly spread and if it is to avoid extinction, which is a very real threat, then urgent action needs to be taken. Fortunately official bodies and volunteer groups in the county and elsewhere are active in various ways to protect this precious animal. Squirrels do not hibernate and so can be seen at any time of year.

Hares, Rabbits and Foxes

The brown hare (*Lepus europaeus*) is rare in the region but the native species, mountain hare (*Lepus timidus*) is more likely to be seen. Its favoured habitats are heath moorland, montane grassland, new forestry plantations and dry, rocky hills. Rabbit (*Orytolagus cuniculus*) was introduced in the 12th century following the Norman Conquest of England.

It is highly adaptable although it prefers loose, free-draining soil with scrub and rocks for cover. It can also be found in small fields, arable or pasture, with hedgerows and in sand dunes. It avoids coniferous woodlands, damp areas and very rarely occurs above the tree line. The red fox (*Vulpes vulpes*) is another very adaptable mammal, living anywhere from sand dunes to mountain tops, and in recent times, urban areas. It is mainly found in a fairly narrow line of territory from Brown Carrick Hill to Galloway Forest Park.

Rare and Not-so-Rare

Badger (*Meles meles*) is an elusive, nocturnal creature with a sparse distribution in Carrick. But its past haunts can be traced through place-names with the element *brock*, the Scots word for badger. Its main habitats are moorland, lowland pastures and natural caves. A very rare animal in the region is the pine marten (*Martes martes*) which has two main distribution points at the extreme north and south of Carrick. Much more widespread are the genus-related stoat (*Mustela erminea*) and weasel (*Mustela nivalis*).

Deer

Roe deer

The largest native mammal in the country is red deer (*Cervus elaphus*) which inhabits upland forests and moorlands. It is likely that Carrick's population is made up of escapees from deer parks. Sika deer (*Cervus Nippon*) can be found in many parts of the region. Its habitats include conifer plantations and farmland, as well as deciduous and mixed woodland with dense undergrowth, on damp ground where the soil is acidic. The small, elegant Roe deer (*Capreolus capreolus*) can be seen in open, deciduous, mixed or coniferous woodlands and moorland.

Carrick's diverse landscapes have gifted the region with a rich variety of fauna on land, sea and in the air. With land mammals ranging from the *wee, sleekit, cowrin, tim'rous beastie* of the mouse to the stately stags with their proud antlers, visitors and residents alike can be grateful that these creatures are there to be enjoyed and respected. It will indeed be a rare thing to see again antlers being turned into light fittings as happened in the 16th century castle of Sanquhar-Hamilton.

13 CASTLES & TOWERS

"The very suggestion that the country seat in Scotland might just be vernacular, rather than designed like the bulk of country houses elsewhere, demonstrates just how deep-seated had become the perception that the Renaissance had eluded Scotland's architecture."

Charles McKean,
The Scottish Chateau; the Country House of Renaissance Scotland, 2001

Pinwherry Castle: conjectural reconstruction by Keith Dawdry

The word *castle* can be confusing for those wishing to grasp the context of the many and varied historical houses of Carrick. One of the most important is called Cassillis (pronounced *castles*) which has a Scots language plural of *is* perhaps because of the proximity of the ancient fort of Dunree. Cassillis House, seat of the Kennedy family, is remarkable for several reasons, not least that it has been inhabited since the late 14th century. The original keep, with walls up to 4 metres thick in places, has been modified over the years. The greatest change was the addition of a large, 19th century mansion attached to the south-east corner.

The only true castles in Carrick are, arguably, Loch Doon and Robert the Bruce's Turnberry. The use of the word castle in the 16th and 17th century was, in fact, a fairly rare occurrence. It was more often than not a statement of status. The subtle difference between castle, keep, fortalice, palace (or place), mansion and tower is nowadays a subject for architectural historians but was meaningful in the past.

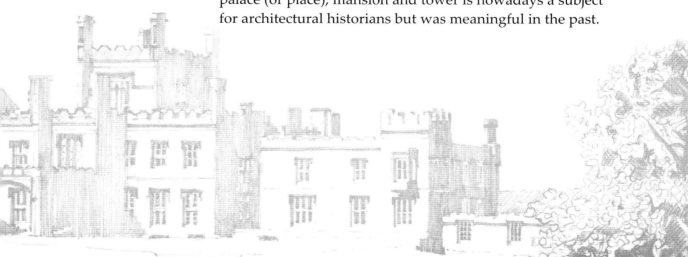

It is worth noticing that each carried a strict legal definition, so that when we read in the testament of Lady Row of Baltersan that it was *"signed at my dwellinghouse"* it informs us that this was not the tower-house we see today.

Loch Doon Castle is now an oddity; forlornly crouching by the shore of the loch. Its irregular polygonal shape originally stood on an island but was removed stone by stone and re-erected on the shore as part of a reservoir building scheme. Dating from the 13th century, it was probably built by the Bruce earls of Carrick. In 1306 it was captured by the English who also attacked Turnberry that year. In an atlas of 1654, based on late 16th century drawings, Loch Doon Castle is shown with another structure to the south of it, used for housing prisoners. The castle is a Scheduled Ancient Monument and is open all year with free entry.

In the same atlas, published in Amsterdam by Joan Blaeu, the world's foremost map-makers, Turnberry Castle is indicated by four tall towers. Just as Renfrewshire and Ayrshire compete for the birthplace of William Wallace, Turnberry and Lochmaben joust for the honour of being the cradle of Robert the Bruce. Sadly there are but a few fragments of wall to be seen today. Its site is picked out for miles around by the lighthouse, established in 1873 by the renowned *"Lighthouse Stevensons"*, and familiar to golfers across the globe.

Another two houses which have had mixed fortunes are masterpieces by neo-classical architect Robert Adam. Culzean was built around the core of an earlier tower-house in masterly fashion between 1777 and 1792 for David Kennedy, 10th Earl of Cassillis. Nowadays the National Trust for Scotland welcomes hundreds of thousands of visitors to the castle, its impressive carriage houses, home farm and beautifully kept gardens and policies.

Far right: Detail from the Blaeu atlas, 1654 shows Loch Doon Castle and prisoners' island at the south end of the loch.

Right: the castle in the 19th c. before its removal to the shore.

Less visible and less fortunate is Adam's other mansion, also built for Kennedys: Thomas and his wife, Jean, who was Adam's niece. On this occasion, the option of extending or converting the 15th century castle of Old Dalquharran was rejected in favour of a new building on an elevated site by the Water of Girvan, near Dailly. Like Culzean, it had a dramatic staircase, a swirling cantilever lit from above. Its compact form was greatly enlarged in 1881 with side wings. Although sensitively applied, they rob us of Adam's original concept. As recently as 1968 Dalquharran was unroofed and the elements accelerated the work of neglect in reducing it to a ragged shell. All that could be comfortably removed, including floors and stair railings, has been stripped away. Yet, the stonework survives in excellent condition as testament to its quality and the work of the masons, some of whom have literally left their personal marks.

Scotland's greatest contribution to Europe's architectural history is the tower-house. Although a common form elsewhere in the continent, the variety of ingenuity and flair employed by Scottish masons is remarkable. At the peak of their popularity in the 16th century, there were perhaps 7,000 of them but today only about 1,000 survive, of which just over 30 are in Carrick. Some have been absorbed into mansion houses such as Culzean. Others have been reduced to mere heaps of stone. A few are still inhabited: Penkill, twice rescued from ruin, and Killochan among the foremost examples.

Dalquarran New & Old

Far right: The late 17th c. entrance and staircase to the old castle which incorporates work from an earlier period. The Latin motto above the doorway reads, *"Ut Scriptura sonat finis non pugna coronat"*.

Right: The stonework of the 1790 new castle by Robert Adam remains in remarkably good condition in spite of the mansion lying empty for years.

Penkill, beside the Penwhapple Burn by Old Dailly, was reconstructed in a fairly heavy-handed way by a 19th century Glasgow architect for Spencer and Alice Boyd, descendents of the original inhabitants and respectively, a carver and a painter. Alice had a love affair with the artist and poet, William Bell Scott (1811-1890) and, as cover for his prolonged and frequent visits to Penkill (he was married), he painted a magnificent medieval-style mural, *The King's Quair* (a love poem by James II), on the stairwell there. Bell brought a string of poets and Pre-Raphaelite artists to Penkill including Dante Gabriel Rossetti, Christina Rossetti, William Holman Hunt and Arthur Hughes.

The common historical process of itinerant artisans and masons moving round the country through family connections appears to be borne out by four particular towers; Baltersan, Killochan, Pinwherry and Park (Glenluce). A now-faded inscription above the entrance to Baltersan stated that it was begun in 1584 by John Kennedy of Pennyglen and his spouse, Margaret Cathcart of Killochan. Two years later Margaret's brother, John Cathcart of Carleton, started work on Killochan with a similar ground plan to Baltersan. A little further south is another former Kennedy home, Pinwherry, dating from around 1596. Near Glenluce Abbey, Galloway, is the House of Park which, like Killochan, retains its entrance lintel inscription. It informs us that Thomas Hay and Janet McDowall had the house built in 1590. Kennedy of Baltersan's third wife was Florence McDowall, just one of numerous marriages and business contacts between various branches of these prominent south-west families.

Top Left: Initials of
Alice Boyd

Far left: Memorial to
William Bell Scott

Left: Portrait of
William Bell Scott

The main architectural feature which unites three of them is the square stair turret in the inner angle of these L-plan towers. At Glenluce, as is normal in Scotland, the turret is rounded, otherwise its external appearance and internal layout resemble Baltersan. Another unusual feature shared by Glenluce, Killochan and Baltersan is a square window with a deep embrasure. Since windows in tower-houses were almost always vertical, usually in a ratio of 1:2 or 1:3, it is a puzzle as to why this quirk was introduced. In each case it would allow sunlight to fall on the great hall fireplace, the focal point of the home.

Baltersan and Pinwherry are in ruins but Killochan has never suffered the misfortune of being abandoned. Instead it has been sensitively extended over the years without detracting from the solidity and grandeur of the main L-plan tower-house. Viewed from Old Dailly it is a most handsome feature in the Girvan valley. It is privately owned and there is no public access.

Some ruined towers stand beside 18th or 19th century mansions and this is often a deliberate decision to retain the ancient pile. It is believed that, just as the great round tower, or *donjon* is the symbol of lordship in France, the old keep is proof of a family's ancient lineage. Others have fared less well and stand alone in gentle decay. Greenan is the most dramatic as it teeters on the edge of a high cliff near the Heads of Ayr.

Detail of oak panels from Killochan, now in the Museum of Scotland, Edinburgh; originally painted in bright colours, they depict John Cathcart of Carleton and his spouse, Helen Wallace (late 16th century).

Killochan (*private*) Note that the square window still retains its 16th century protective grille.

A little further down the coast are the ruins of Dunure Castle, considered the fount of the various Kennedy family lines. Its most distinctive feature now is the very rare beehive-shaped dovecot matching one at Crossraguel Abbey. A less happy connection with the abbey is the notorious roasting of the abbey commendator there by Gilbert, 4th Earl of Cassillis. On the hillside above Dunure is an inhabited tower that was neither restored nor reconstructed. Dunduff has the distinction of being the only surviving tower-house to be abandoned mid-construction. It lay that way until the 20th century when it was completed as a private dwellinghouse.

"When I look at that splendid 'Land of Burns' which adorns my shelves — & recollect sundry precious prints I am abashed by the contrast of the little I have given with the greatness of what I have received." **Lord Cockburn**, distinguished advocate and judge, writing to D.O. Hill in 1847.

Etching of Dunure by the world-famous pioneering photographer, **David Octavius Hill** for his book, *Land of Burns,* published in Glasgow in 1840.

A few miles to the east is another very rare survival in the town of Maybole. Although known as Maybole Castle, it was the town house of the Kennedys of Cassillis and has remained occupied for various uses by the family since it was built in the mid-16th century to the present day. It is one of about 20 such buildings which once stood along the High Street of Maybole as town houses for various lairds who would have found travel in winter both difficult and dangerous because this was a time of regular family feuds. The only other survivor, once owned by the Kennedys of Blairquhan, is now incorporated into the fabric of the town hall.

Close by the road from Culzean to Maidens are the squat, cracked and broken remains of Thomaston, a home of the McIlvanes of Grimmet which was occupied down to 1800. This is a comparatively late date for a tower-house to survive. There are other empty shells at Kirkhill (Colmonell) and Knockdolian which simply went out of fashion as the main houses of small estates in the mid-18th century.

A century later, revival became the order of the day with conjectural restorations such as the charming house of Kilhenzie (pronounced *Kilheeny*) at the centre of a busy farm, or substantial additions like Cassillis, Cloncaird and Newark, by Alloway. All remain private dwellings and are not open to the public.

Cloncaird, by Kirkmichael, the only example in Ayrshire of a style based on English and Welsh castles of Edward I of England. Built on to an old tower-house in 1814 by an unknown architect, possibly Robert Wallace who bid unsuccessfully for the remodelling of Blairquhan in 1819.

In 1563 Mary, Queen of Scots, toured Carrick to raise support among the powerful Kennedys and their allies. Her progress, involving upwards of 400 people, effectively her whole household and bodyguards, would have been a topic of conversation for generations. From Dunure she made her way to Ardmillan, just south of Girvan and on to Ardstinchar at Ballantrae. Here would have been a most poignant visit as it would be a vivid reminder of Mary's time as Queen of France.

For the castle was built about a hundred years earlier by Hew Kennedy, known as *Hew, come-with-the-penny*. He spent years in the service of Charles VII of France and earned his nickname when he returned to Scotland with great riches and permission from the French king to include the *fleur de lys* in his coat of arms. His exploits included military action with the large contingent of Scots in the army of Joan of Arc at the Relief of Orleans in 1429. He was also present in the French army which defeated the English at Baugé in 1421 and at Verneuil three years later when the English were victorious. Today, Ardmillan is totally gone and Ardstinchar is but a finger of stone like a sentinel above the pretty village of Ballantrae.

The castles and towers of Carrick each have tales to tell but it is wrong to think of them as the scenes of sieges and mayhem. Certainly, some were the focal points of petty, and occasional bloody feuds. But for the most part they were simply the family seat: the centre of an estate of subsistence farmers where the laughter of children would mingle with the grumbles of weary field workers. The real battles were with the ever-changing and unforgiving climate.

Arms of Kennedy of Ardstinchar whose castle stood above the village of Ballantrae (*pictured left*)

14 CARRICK AT WORK

"And yet, as it seemed to me typical of much that is evil in Scotland, Maybole is also typical of much that is best. Some of the factories were originally founded and are still possessed by self-made men of the sterling, stout old breed – fellows who made some little bit of an invention, borrowed some little pocketful of capital, and then, step by step, in courage, thrift, and industry, fought their way upwards to an assured position."

Robert Louis Stevenson (1850 – 1894),
A Winter's Walk in Carrick and Galloway, 1876.

Ayrshire cow:
One of the world's
great breeds

At the end of the last Ice Age, 8-10,000 years ago, Scotland would have resembled the landscape of present-day Iceland. The retreating glaciers left behind boulder-strewn valleys and hundreds of lochs. Gradually vegetation formed as lichens, mosses, juniper and heather clothed the countryside and great forests spread. The first settlers in Carrick, which was easily accessible from the Bay of Biscay via the Irish Sea and the Firth of Clyde, would have depended upon wild animals, fish, fruit and nuts for sustenance. These Mesolithic hunter-gatherers would have found survival a full-time occupation so there would have been no time or adequate human resources to build great temples, forts or monuments as their descendents did.

The Neolithic or New Stone Age started about 4,000 years ago and saw the dawn of farming as animals and plants introduced from mainland Europe became the sources of food. New technologies arrived in the form of pottery, tools and weapons. Forests were cleared and soils were enriched through hundreds of years of natural and man-made intervention. Traces of these early peoples remain throughout Carrick with hill forts at Kildoon by Maybole,

Hollowsheen (Kirkoswald), Dowhill and Hadyard Hill (both near Girvan), and one of the best preserved in all Scotland, Dinvin by Pinmore.

Farming to 1700

From those ancient times to about 1700, farming changed little in the Lowlands of Scotland. The system of land tenure that evolved whereby families could only have a maximum tack (lease) of 19 years discouraged any long-term investment in holdings. Farm buildings were insubstantial huddles of heather-thatched, clay-walled hovels. The most valuable items were the wooden crucks or roof timbers which could be transported to a new smallholding, giving rise to the phrase *to up sticks*, meaning to move on.

In the days before proper land drainage (and place-name evidence tells us Scotland was a wet place) a system of co-operative land management came into being. Known as run-rig, the land was formed into strips of ground separated by ditches. The purpose was to give everyone a fair share of the good and bad soil. However it meant a farmer could

William Douglas, farmer at Monkwood Mains, Minishant, ploughing with a four horse team in 1941. Courtesy of www.maybole.org

have his crops and beasts scattered across a wide area interspersed with the property of several neighbours. It was inefficient and led to many quarrels and court cases.

Poverty and food shortages were commonplace, with famine striking about once every generation. Social conditions were wretched but there would have been some compensation in the self-sufficiency of the settlements known as *fermtouns*. These brought together various tradesmen such as the shoemaker, wheelwright, weaver, basket maker and others important to agriculture. In a society with little cash in circulation, bartering would have been common currency. More specialist needs would have been available on the nearest estate or within the parish.

Given the power of the landowners – mainly the titled heritors and the Church pre-1560, and post-Reformation, a broader swathe of 'bonnet' lairds and *guidmen* – security of tenure was surprisingly good for the humble farmers. A system of customary inheritance known as *kindly tenure* was developed and became an assumption, a right even in some people's minds, that a holding could pass to someone who could claim their nearest kin had farmed the land. Lawyers' protocol books (a day book record of legal cases) are peppered with disputes on this subject and farmers often triumphed against powerful earls.

The 1530 testament of Egidia Blair, Lady Row of Baltersan (a small estate beside Crossraguel Abbey) is a wonderful social history document as it is filled with legacies and an inventory of crops and beasts.

"Imprimis. I confess myself to have sixty-one cows, the price of the piece two merks, *summa* eighty-two pounds. *Item,* twenty-nine oxen, the price of each, thirty shillings, *sum,* forty-three pounds ten shillings. *Item,* fifteen two year olds, the price per piece one merk, *sum* ten pounds. *Item,* nine sterks, the price per piece eight shillings, *sum,* three pounds twelve shillings. *Item,* five hundred and forty-three sheep, the price per piece five shillings, *sum,* one hundred and sixty-two pounds ten shillings. *Item,* fourscore and ten lambs, the price of the piece sixteen pennies, *sum,* six pounds. *Item,* in victual, *viz.,* in bere [an ancient type of barley] and meal, one hundred and eighty-two bolls, the price of the boll twelve shillings, *sum,* one hundred and twenty-one pounds four shillings. *Item,* one hundred and sixty bolls oats, the price of the boll twelve shillings, *sum,* fifty-four pounds. *Item,* horses, mares, and stags in the muir, the price of them all, thirty pounds. *Item,* in utensils and domicills, forty pounds. *Item,* for the rents and profits of Row, twenty pounds."

Alexander Jack & Sons product

© Alistair Hastings

One legacy shows farm improvement was uppermost in her mind:
"If the money given out and bequeathed by me to the said John Whytefurd and David Hynd, be not laid out upon land within two years for the use and profit of the said John Whytefurd ...."

The redistribution of Church land before and after the Reformation led in some cases to the establishment of new estates and to sub-divisions of holdings which we can see today in farm names prefixed with Easter and Wester, Nether and Over, Laigh and High.

The country estate

The first gardening book written for the Scottish climate was published in 1683. The author, John Reid, was gardener at Niddry Castle near Edinburgh where his father and grandfather had been gardeners. Although Niddry fell into ruin, the high walls of Reid's garden still stand. The castle was restored in recent times as a private home.

On an estate the two most important members of staff were the gardener and the cook. There is a false belief that food in 18th century Scotland was plain and boring. A mere glance at Reid's book blows that myth away. And yet the range of fruits, vegetables and herbs he deals with should come as no surprise. A 1559 inventory of the castle of Sanquhar-Hamilton in Ayr lists:

"2 large orchards and yards having 3 gates and planted with stands of hawthorn bushes, gooseberry bushes, redcurrant bushes, rose bushes, apple trees, plum trees, cherry trees, wild plum trees, almond trees, plane trees, birch trees, ash, hawthorn and other trees and provided with two ponds."

In his introduction to a 2004 facsimile edition of Elizabeth Cleland's 1755 cookery book, Peter Brears says,

"In the 18th century, there were three very distinct culinary traditions operating in Scotland. At the highest level came the cooking of the great noble families, who required the very finest of international cuisine. Next came the cookery of the gentry and merchant classes .... wholesome and varied ....The remaining type of cookery was that used by the country's working population .... they made the very best of local ingredients .... gave rise to considerable ingenuity, however, thus producing a highly individual tradition of true Scottish cookery, one of the most interesting of all Europe's national cuisines."

The 18th century was a period of considerable land improvements by the country estates. As new drainage systems increased the land available for agriculture, the unearthed stones created drystane dykes to better contain sheep and cattle as well as give us the countryside we recognise today. New methods and machinery were being introduced, making food production more efficient. Exploitation of minerals brought about by the industrial revolution increased the wealth of the estate owners who abandoned their tower-houses for new, large mansions designed by a new bread of craftsmen – classical architects. These high-status properties required a large number of servants to run them.

Country estates like Cassillis, Blairquhan, Kilkerran, Killochan and many others throughout Carrick were important providers of employment for people remote from industrial Glasgow and Lanarkshire. Although the high point of houses having armies of servants passed with the First World War, life "downstairs" is still within living memory for a number of people in Carrick today.

To a conservation-minded society it is unthinkable that so many historic mansions became the plaything of army training. The late James Hunter Blair of Blairquhan used to recall dinner table conversations when owners would ask each other, *"When is your house being blown up?"*

The history of Blairquhan is fairly typical of the changing fortunes of families over the centuries. The old courtyard castle dated back to 1346 when the McWhirters were the first occupants. Around 1573 it was inherited by Kennedys who extended the property. Within a few decades the Whitefoords took over. Around 1760 the castle was rented by the McAdams of Lagwyne, parents of the famous road builder, John Loudon McAdam, who was raised at Blairquhan and attended school in Maybole six miles away. But the Whitefoords suffered in the collapse in 1773 of Douglas, Heron & Company, the Ayr bank. Five years later they sold Blairquhan to Sir David Hunter Blair whose descendents have lived there to this day.

In 1821 the old castle was swept away. Although a few interesting pieces of Renaissance stonework which resemble parts of Maybole Castle, were incorporated into the gothic pile Sir David commissioned from the architect, William Burn. One of the many delights of Blairquhan is that there have been no major alterations or additions to the fabric or furnishings of the castle since it was completed in 1824. Apart from the maturity of the grounds planned by Sir David, we can see what he and his architect saw.

What we will not see, of course, are 18 resident servants as Sir David had back then although there still is a community caring for the castle and policies and Blairquhan continues to contribute to Carrick's economy through tourism. Life for servants could be extremely harsh and certainly low-paid although this would be balanced by benefits in kind such as accommodation, food and clothing. It certainly suited Thomas Burnie who died in 1855 at the age of 75, having been butler at Blairquhan for 46 years. A full and fascinating account of life in service is given by Jean Aitchison in her Ayrshire monograph, *Servants in Ayrshire 1750-1914.*

The first houses in the classical style in Carrick were Kilkerran and Ardmillan. The former has been greatly altered. The latter was allowed to fall into despairing ruin and then ignominiously demolished – a great loss to Ayrshire.

The Georgian period produced Cloncaird, by Kirkmichael, and the great works of Robert Adam at Dalquharran and Culzean. This was followed by the English manorial style, as at Blairquhan, and the much-derided mock-Elizabethan and Scotch Baronial. Gradually the old estates, which depended upon agriculture and then forestry, quarrying, lime, coal and salt pans for their income, were being challenged for high status by rich industrialists who still liked the idea of large policies around their mansions and a life of rural leisure.

Maybole factory of Alexander Jack & Sons
Picture courtesy of www.maybole.org

JACK'S IMPLEMENT WORKS 1840

Thomas Burnie: butler, Blairquhan by W. Crawford, ARSA, 1849

Farming in the 19th and 20th centuries

As farm machinery became more readily available, production increased, as did the prosperity of the farmers. By the 1890s Glasgow was, on a *per capita* basis, the richest city in the world, creating massive demand for foodstuffs. The Glasgow to Ayr railway line opened in 1840 and was extended to Maybole by 1856 and four years later to Girvan. By 1877 Barrhill was connected by train to Girvan.

The need for agricultural implements led to the growth of Alexander Jack & Sons of Maybole. Their works designed and made a variety of farming tools such as potato grubbers, rakes, and manure spreaders. They also made hay carts and milk floats. The company was founded in 1852 and employed 150 people by 1905. It closed down in the 1960s and the factory was demolished in 2009.

Girvan, 12 miles south of Maybole, was the main centre of Ayrshire potato production. The light soils there saw the first growth of early potatoes in the middle of the 19th century. By the 1930s Girvan had a virtual monopoly of the Scottish early potato market. Production became extensive throughout Ayrshire but on some farms it was incredibly intensive. A field at Jameston, by Maidens, had, by 1900, been under early potatoes for 37 successive years. In 1913 a field at nearby Morriston beat that by one year and by 1958 another field there reached its 70th consecutive year. After the Second World War the number of Irish potato

Trees Farm, Maybole
© Fred Westcott

The place-name is from Cumbric (Old Welsh) *tre*, a settlement.

diggers, known as "tattie howkers", declined. For generations, these itinerant workers were a prominent sight in Carrick and elsewhere in Scotland from mid-June to early August. There has been no decline, however, in the quality and popularity of Ayrshire potatoes, which are now renowned far beyond Carrick.

Sheep rearing

In 1923 nearly 260 farms in Carrick had been issued with sheep marks. Almost half of these were in the parishes of Barr and Colmonell. However by the 1970s, sheep were making way for forestry, and annual social events such as the Shepherds' Fair in Barr came to an end. The Shepherds' Fair could be lively but it never reached the excesses recorded for the notorious Kirkdandy Fair which took place on the last Sunday of May at an ancient church one and a half miles south-west of the village. It was a "feeing" or hiring fair where agricultural workers sought employment. The day started early with business matters such as selling sheep or bartering wool and other gear. As the hours passed and the merrymaking increased, needless to say it often ended in tumult, hangovers and, as Robert Burns observed elsewhere in Ayrshire, *houghmagandie*.

Sheep farming has been in long-term decline throughout Scotland but, as the forests are harvested, leaving bare, scarred hillsides, it begs the question of what will replace the trees. In some places it is the latest wind turbine technology that

Stinchar Valley

63

provides the economic input to the community while generating hostility and admiration in what appears to be equal measure.

Ayrshire cattle

The sturdy black cattle that were fattened in the fields of Carrick and driven to markets in the North of England, gave way in the 19th century to the distinctive white and reddish-brown Ayrshire breed which is now world-famous. However, they in turn were largely supplanted by the ubiquitous black and white Friesians and Holsteins which offered higher milk yields.

Originally Ayrshires sported magnificent upright horns but nowadays they are so charming and doe-eyed that some farmers keep the odd beast or two as pets the way others are attracted to the shaggy, Highland breed as adornments rather than "cash cows" so to speak. Although a minority breed, their numbers are rising as farmers realise the ratio of feed to milk yield of Holsteins is time consuming and less economic compared with Ayrshires. The Scottish breed is popular with organic farmers and can thrive in conditions as diverse as Scandinavia and Africa. It is pleasing to know that Prince Charles, Earl of Carrick, keeps a herd of Ayrshires at his country house, Highgrove.

Coal mining

The earliest written record of coal in Scotland is in a charter granted in 1291 to the Abbot and Convent of Dunfermline, but it is believed that the first exploiters of the mineral were the monks of Newbattle Abbey near Edinburgh. A Papal envoy, Aeneas Silvius Piccolomini (1405-1464), later Pope Pius II (1458-1464), visited Scotland and was astonished to see people burning stones, as he thought. Several charters of Crossraguel Abbey in the 1560s mention the monks right to extract coal from the *coal-heuchs* and *coal-pottis* of Yellowlie and other places in that district. It is highly probable that coal heated the abbey many years before then. The monks' source was probably what became known as Dalzellolie pit. The letter "z" is the old Scots letter *yogh* which was pronounced as "y". This pit caught fire in 1749 then burned for around 100 years.

In 1750 Lady Kennedy, mother of Sir Thomas, 9th Earl of Cassillis, summoned engineer James Scott, who was working at Kilkerran, to explore for coal at Culzean where excavations were also planned to find limestone.

Ayrshire was second in importance after Lanarkshire for coal mining in Scotland. Within Carrick, Dailly was the focus of activity with mines on the Bargany and Dalquharran estates. In 1896 Dalquharran pit employed over 100 workers. More than 100 mines were operating at one time or another but the industry eventually declined and the last pit, Dalquharran, closed in 1977.

Today there is almost no trace on the surface that such an important industry existed. However, there is a remarkable survival south of Girvan Station in an early 20th century "pit village" of houses built by the Killochan Coal Co. Ltd and its successor, South Ayrshire Collieries Ltd.

Fishing

In the 19th century when Scotland had the biggest fishing fleet in Europe, huge shoals of herring arrived every winter to spawn off the south coast of Arran and at Ballantrae Banks. Small rowing and sailing skiffs were the preferred craft. In summer when the herring were not in shoals, other catches were made including mackerel, cod, haddock, whiting, turbot and flounders.

The Ballantrae herring fisheries were by 1870 the most important in Scotland, with vessels even arriving from east coast ports, making use of the Caledonian Canal. At this time the main types of nets were the drift, trammel and seine. Trammel nets had been used in the Firth of Clyde for centuries, but gradually the more prodigious seine net came to prominence. In 1890 over 900 fishermen were employed at Ballantrae.

Abundant catches were not guaranteed; there were good years and bad years. The Revd Abercrombie, writing in 1686 about the importance of the Ballantrae herring fishing at Christmas, recalls *"but that has ceased some thirty years past."*

Today, Girvan with only six fishing boats sailing out of it, is the only recognised fish-landing port in Carrick. The smaller harbours such as Ballantrae, Maidens and Dunure have fallen out of commercial use. However, Ballantrae still retains its status as a port of registry for fishing vessels with the letters BA.

Smuggling

For an illegal and frequently violent trade, there is a surprising amount of detailed documentary evidence of smuggling. Until the Treaty of Union in 1707, the collection of import and export duties in Scotland was in the hands of merchants acting on behalf of the Crown. The establishment of customs and excise officers, combined with the tea import monopoly held by the English East India Company, gave rise to a widespread trade in contraband along the coasts of Ireland, England, Wales and Scotland, with the Isle of Man at its centre. High-price tea, high import duties, high demand, adaptable merchants and anti-Union sentiment in Scotland combined to energise and grow an economic network which involved everyone from the children of farm labourers to the highest of the landed gentry. Fortunes were there to be made and lost.

Anything subject to an import duty could be smuggled, including wine, brandy, rum, tobacco and even Barcelona handkerchiefs. The links in the chain of supply started with the producer's agent selling goods to middlemen who broke no laws when they sold on to the smugglers who transported the contraband by boats known as wherries. These vessels landed their cargoes on dark, moonless nights and certainly not into caves, as popular imagination would have us believe. Instead, large groups, often including servants from notable country houses, quickly distributed the casks, boxes and sacks to a multitude of hiding places away from the coast, awaiting delivery to the final link in the chain, the customers.

Girvan Harbour

An incident near Culzean Bay on Sunday, 21st October, 1764 is vividly described by Frances Wilkins in her compelling book, *The Smuggling Trade Revisited*. It involved a Manx boat which struck a rock about 300 yards from shore, causing the crew to jettison some casks. Word spread rapidly and churchgoers in Kirkoswald hurried to the shore to help, and to help themselves to the jetsam. Ebenezer and Thomas Ferguson secured a cask each and their servants made their way to seize the boat. Instead they were ordered by the revenue men to help James McMicken, a customs officer, known as a tidesman, from Turnberry.

Meanwhile, other men and women arrived with horses and carts from Ardlochan, Balsarroch, Caldwell, Drumgerloch, Shanter, Morriston and Dalquhat. Several revenue men launched a small boat to unload the rest of the cargo while others remained on shore to gather the casks washed on to the beach. They ordered bystanders to assist but at least a dozen refused to do so. Although most of the casks, known as ankers, each with a capacity of 10 gallons, were seized, a number still reached the smugglers' customers.

The inevitable outcome was a kirk session enquiry at Kirkoswald for those who breached the Sabbath to admit their guilt and seek forgiveness. Needless to say, that did not hamper the lucrative trade of smuggling. Indeed, the parish of Kirkoswald was the base for the most important group of smugglers in Carrick, operating as William Breckenridge & Co.

Although long stretches of the Carrick shore are rocky, there are a number of beaches, such as Culzean Bay and further south where the Lady Burn enters the sea by Drumgerloch, which were frequently used as landing-places. But one Carrick smuggling story that doesn't hold water is the famous legend of Sawney Bean and his family of cannibals in a cave at Balcreuchan Port between Lendalfoot and Ballantrae. There is no documentary evidence for the existence

Dick Goudie
(1912-2002):
the last boot maker in Maybole with a pair of the famous Maybole *tackettie* boots

67

of these ferocious troglodytes. Smugglers may have used caves, but only to shelter from inclement weather and certainly not to store contraband. Nevertheless, Sawney remains an unshakeable part of popular folklore. He is even honoured by the Ordnance Survey which clearly marks the Bean house on its Landranger map of the district. But he is not alone, for another notorious extended family, the Gubbins of Lydford on Dartmoor, south-west England, also supposedly terrorised travellers in the 16th and 17th centuries. They, like Sawney and his relatives, came to an apocryphal bloody end.

Boot and shoe industry

In 1838 Maybole saw the start of an industry that would turn handloom weavers into leather workers. When John Gray & Co opened their factory they could hardly have imagined the growth that this small town would experience. By 1901, the boot and shoe industry in Maybole (population 5,470) employed 1,645 people in nine factories. The town's main product was heavy-duty boots with soles and heels studded with metal tickets, hence the name *tacketties*. As with so much in life, fashions changed and competitors produced lighter footwear. Production peaked in the 1890s and by 1924 the workforce had dropped to 530. The factories have been demolished and the industry has now become a part of the town's history.

Maybole: Kirkwynd boot and shoe factory with Maybole Castle in the background.

15 PAGANS & SAINTS

"Clemens episcopus servus servorum Dei dilectis filiis abbati monasterii sancti Jacobi et sancti Mirini confessoris de Passelet eisque fratribus tam presentibus quam futuris regularem vitam professis imperpetuum ... Ex dono Duncani comitis de Karric totam terram de Crosragmol et Suthblan cum pertinentiis suis ..."

Bull by Pope Clement IV, confirming to the monks of Paisley sundry lands and churches; among them the whole land of Crossraguel and Southblane in Carrick with their pertinents (associated rights and properties), by the gift of **Duncan, Earl of Carrick**, 1269.

The Glake Stone: An ancient cup-marked stone at the summit of a hill above Pinwherry by the source of the Glake Burn. It may have formed part of a chambered cairn about 20 metres in diameter.

Below:
An incised stone from Machar-a-kill near Kilkerran. It was possibly the base for a cross. Detail from Blaeu atlas (1654).

About five millennia before Duncan, Earl of Carrick, instructed Paisley Abbey to found a daughter house of the Order of Cluny at Crossraguel, the first farmers were reshaping the landscape and society. Customs, rituals and mutual obligations were established to maintain order in communities that were increasingly complex and interdependent or competitive and hostile. There was a need for ceremonial sites for marriages, funerals and marking significant dates in the calendar such as the equinoxes and solstices. The use of geometry and the passing of time were combined with the observation of the movement of the sun, moon and stars which told these ancient people when to plant crops or celebrate the changing of the seasons. This in turn led to the establishment of four major festivals in the Celtic year.

The Quarter-Day festivals are Imbolc, Beltane, Lughnasadh and Samhuinn. Imbolc, an Irish Gaelic word meaning "in the belly", marks the early beginnings of spring, with the earth ready to "give birth" to new life. The passing of winter, with its hazards of cold and hunger, would have been a time of relief and hope for ancient peoples. This was followed around the beginning of May by a fire festival called Beltane. Before modern calendars were established it is believed that the blossoming of hawthorn was the signal for this festival to take place. The arrival of summer and new growth in crops and beasts would have been a joyous time.

The harvest festival of Lughnasadh (pronounced *Loo-nasah*), meaning the "corn king", is also of Irish origin. In Scotland it is known as Lammas, which is derived from old English, meaning "loaf mass". It is claimed that it was a popular time for a form of irregular (and trial) marriage called "handfasting" whereby a couple pledged to remain together for a year and a day, by which time they would decide if the relationship had a future. This "tradition" though is questionable in its extent and antiquity, and owes more to mythology than reality. A form of it, "irregular marriage by declaration *de presenti*", did exist in Scotland until 1940 when it was no longer recognised as lawful. Samhuinn (pronounced *Sa-wayne*) was the Celtic New Year marking the approach of winter. It was the time to bring the herds into enclosures for protection. As vegetation died away, it was believed to be a time for mischievous and evil spirits to emerge; a superstition which evolved into the festival of Hallowe'en. The exact nature of ancient ceremonies and spirituality cannot be judged by

Girvan Festival of Light: a fabulous community event drawing upon ancient traditions
Picture courtesy of CRAG Carrick Rural Arts Group

modern interpretations such as Beltane in Edinburgh which is a tourist attraction attended by over 10,000 paying onlookers. Hard archaeological evidence can only tell us so much, and there is a fair scattering of that across Carrick in the form of cairns, burial mounds and standing stones. Modern farming and urban development has, of course, obliterated many sites. In Girvan a road overlays a burial ground of the Middle Bronze Age. But in the south-west of the region there is a significant survival of three monuments atop Finnarts Hill, by Glen App. Between standing stones and a cairn is what is believed to be a henge, which is a roughly circular or oval-shaped enclosure surrounded by a ditch and external bank with one or two entrances, suggesting that it was for private ceremonies for a select few. Dating from the late Neolithic period, henges are believed to have replaced the earlier burial mounds as the focal points of religious life in what may have been the development of a more hierarchical society with individual burials for important "chiefs" or elite members of the community.

Crossraguel Abbey: carved oak panels found in a neighbouring farm by Ayr architect James A. Morris at the beginning of the 20th century. Note the serpent on the far left proffering a fruit. The leaves appear to be those of the tomato plant, known in the 16th century as the *"love apple"*.

© Abal Studios, East Kilbride

Although we know little of these pagan times their standing stones remain in places such as Lyonstone farm by Maybole, Turnberry and at Garleffin, just south of Ballantrae. But one of the most intriguing is the carving of a pagan symbol of fertility, a "green man", in Crossraguel Abbey. The arrival and spread of Christianity in Carrick would have been strongly guided by the early Irish saints and, from his base at Whithorn, by St Ninian, a Galwegian. The influence of these holy men can be traced through place-names with Ninian being commemorated at Killantringan which is a very interesting Gaelic/Scots compound. *Kill* is from Gaelic *cille*, a cell or church, and *Tringan* is derived from the Scots *Sanct Ringan* (this being the same as St Trinian which has much less pious connotations nowadays).

Other saints' names are found at Auchenblane (*field of Blane*), Balkissock (*town of Kessog or Cessoc*), Ballantrae (*St Cuthbert*, the town was previously known as Kirkcudbright-Innertig – *the church of St Cuthbert at the mouth of the River Tig*), Colmonell (*Colmán Elo*), Crossraguel (*Riaghail*), Kilbride and Kirkbride (*Bridget*), Kildonan (*Donnán*), Kilhenzie (*Cainneach Mocu Dalon*), Kilkerran (*Ciaran*), Killochan (*Onchú*), Kilphin (*Finnén*), Kilwhannel (possibly *Connel*), Kilpatrick, Kirkmichael, Kirkoswald, Machar-a-kill, by Kilkerran (possibly *Machar* or *Macarius*). St Murray near Culroy, seems to go unexplained and virtually unrecorded yet it might be connected with Port Murray, by Maidens. Other clues to the spread of church influence are in the place-name elements of *grange* (monastic store for crops), *mannach* (monk), *saggart* (priest), *cross* and *corse*.

It is in the tranquil, gracious ruins of Crossraguel Abbey that various threads of this story come together. It was founded in the middle of the 13th century by Duncan, the first Earl of Carrick as a daughter house of Paisley Abbey which had been founded in 1163 by Walter Fitz Alan, an Anglo-Breton from Much Wenlock in England. A descendent of Walter started the Stewart dynasty. It was not uncommon for Christian churches to be built on sites that were previously important to pagans and Crossraguel does give an impression of being in a natural amphitheatre with what might be burial mounds (or perhaps glacial drumlins) and a natural spring (important in ancient Celtic folklore) to the west. It is open to the east with a view to distant hills.

The abbey church is oriented about 8 degrees to the north of east and this must have been deliberate, for a small window below the belfry is positioned in such a way that on the 1st May at the time of Vespers, the sunlight shines directly on to the high altar. The church is dedicated to the Virgin Mary, for whom the month is named. The same thing happens on the other side of the summer solstice, 10th August, feast day of Saints Blane and Oswald. Auchenblane and Kirkoswald are within a mile's distance of the abbey. Sunrise on 30th March has the sun in a direct line with the high altar and the belfry window. This date is recorded as the feast day of the 3rd century Greek St Regulus of Senlis (in France) and St Regulus, believed to be a Scottish abbot of the 4th or 6th century. If this date fell within Lent, their feast day was moved to 17th October which is one of three dates recorded for Riaghail, an Irish saint of about the 8th century.

72

It is not unusual for an abbey church to have more than one patron saint; Paisley has St James the Greater of Compostela for the Stewart dynasty, Miren, the local saint and St Milburga of Much Wenlock which supplied the original monks to Paisley. But this new discovery at Crossraguel (which means Cross of Riaghail) deserves deeper investigation.

Prehistoric standing stones have been studied in great depth to establish the significance of their astrological and topographical alignments. Knowledge of geometry and astronomy is very ancient and the original masons who constructed Crossraguel made good use of it. By the late 15th century, when the finest architecture was applied to the abbey's chapter house and sacristy, the master mason placed a carving of a 'green man' in the south-west corner of the sacristy or *sang schule* where the monks would have rehearsed Gregorian chant under an acoustically wonderful vaulted roof. The "green man" is being carefully watched by a triple-faced head in the north-east corner; perhaps a triumph of the Holy Trinity over paganism.

New York Times, 3rd November, 1922

The abbey is half-way between Paisley Abbey and Whithorn; a deliberate act by the Cluniacs whose mission was to encourage pilgrimage. The route via Kilwinning, Crossraguel, Ballantrae and Glenluce to Whithorn has these places each about 25 miles apart. James IV made numerous pilgrimages to Whithorn, including from Paisley. And here, the story comes full circle. His granddaughter, Mary, Queen of Scots, was taken to France for safe-keeping when she was only five years old. At her landing place in Brittany she expressed the devotion of the Stewarts to Ninian by having a small chapel built and dedicated to the Scottish saint at Roscoff. It survived, albeit in ruins, into the 20th century only to be destroyed by some malevolent Breton officials. Perhaps they still carried some of the traits of their paganistic ancestors who sailed to Carrick 9,000 years earlier.

CHAPEL OF MARY STUART.

A Neglected Ruin Whose Recent Destruction Is Small Loss.

To the Editor of The New York Times:

I was interested to read in this morning's paper of the destruction of the Chapel of Mary Stuart in Brittany. This was originally a small but solidly built votive chapel to St. Ninian at Roscoff, which, after passing through the Revolution with little damage, fell gradually into decay, but could easily have been put to use again. The late Marquess of Bute offered to restore it at his own expense, but, the anti-clerical régime of Combes and Clemenceau coming on, he was refused permission to do so, and the local authorities did all that they could to degrade and destroy the venerable ruin.

When I saw it a few years ago, the stones were a quarry, the foundations undermined, the walls still standing, covered with all sorts of vile and vulgar appeals against religion. Stray pigs and cattle made it a common pound. I felt particularly indignant at such an outrage, for Mary Seton, one of the Four Marys, attended the young Queen of Scots to France and passed through Roscoff with her. It is better that St. Ninian's should have passed away and not continue to be an eyesore to the feelings of decent people.

ARCHBISHOP SETON.

Convent, N. J., Nov. 1, 1922.

73

16 MONKS, MARTYRS & MONARCHS

*"In respect we intend to caus build and repair the hous and place of
Corsragwell to the use of our dearest sone the Prince to quhome
the same is maist proper for his residence quhen he salhappin
to resorte in thai pairtes."*

Command dated 21st February, 1602 by **James VI** (1566 – 1625), King of Scots,
wishing to turn Crossraguel Abbey into a palace for Prince Henry. It did not
happen. The following year the king became James I of England and his son died
nine years later, aged 18.

Crossraguel Abbey:
window mullions are
slightly raised as can
be seen in Straiton
Kirk; perhaps the
work of the same
stonemason.

Straiton Kirk: the
south transept (on the
right) dates to 1510,
twenty years before
the window in the
nave of Crossraguel
(above).

James VI perhaps felt his family owned Crossraguel
Abbey, because so many of his Stewart ancestors (and
Bruce ones before them) had been generous benefactors
to this small religious house in the sequestered parish of
Kirkoswald. About the time of the king's claim, the last
monk, John Bryce, died. Monastic life had been allowed to
fade slowly into history after the 1560 Reformation, perhaps
due to the protection of the 4th and 5th Earls of Cassillis.
While the nave was used as a parish church after 1560, the
other buildings fell into decay, a process accelerated by
people taking away building materials for their own
steadings and homes.

Destruction was eventually curtailed in the mid-18th

century by Adam Fergusson of
Kilkerran, although weather and
encroaching vegetation further
reduced the buildings for another
150 years when finally, attention
was properly given to this most
wonderful ancient monument.
Now it is a serene and spiritually
uplifting place in the care of
Historic Scotland.

Carrick can proudly claim to be the crucible, if not the cradle, from which emerged one of Scotland's greatest monarchs, King Robert I, *The Bruce*. He was born either at Lochmaben in Dumfries-shire or at Turnberry. Certainly it was in the latter territory that he started his long battle to recover Scottish sovereignty from the invading English armies of Edward I and his son, Edward II. In 1306 one such army had commandeered Crossraguel Abbey from where Henry de Percy wrote to Sir James Dalileghe seeking two siege engines. A letter from the English king to Dalileghe confirmed that they had been sent to Loch Doon to attack the castle there.

Crossraguel Abbey: a view of the cloister garth from the gatehouse tower

The second monarch of the Stewart dynasty, Robert III, granted the abbey its most important charter in 1404, giving the abbot powers of regality over Crossraguel's extensive lands, a position the senior house, Paisley Abbey did not achieve for another 84 years. The following year a visitation by a delegation from the mother house of Cluny, in Burgundy, reported that 10 monks was the complete establishment of the monastery. The document, in the Bibliothèque Nationale in Paris, states;

"Dénombrement des abbayes, prieurés, et maisons religieuses dépendant médiatement ou immédiatement des abbayes et ordre de Cluny, tant en Angleterre qu'en Ecosse: Item abbatia de Crossagmel Glasguensis diocesis que immediate est subiecta abbatie de Passeleto in qua erant anno Domini M°IIII° quinto X monachi."

Although the abbey never played a significant role in national political life, it has the distinction of being the most complete remains of any medieval monastery in Scotland. Important evidence survives of the various components of abbey life, including the endearing terrace of houses for retired clerics, known as corrodiars. Each dwelling had a generous living and dining area with a fireplace and ingleneuk seats, a private toilet and a bed chamber through the wall from its neighbour's hearth, providing a welcome source of conducted heat. Elsewhere the chapter house and sacristy have fine vaulted ceilings and the high skill of the 15th century masons can also be found in the choir at the polygonal apse, a rare French-inspired feature, where the ornate *sedilia* and *piscina* have miraculously survived.

In 1547 the great personal wealth of Gavin Dunbar, Archbishop of Glasgow, was brought to the abbey for safe-keeping under the trusted care of Abbot William Kennedy. Within nine months both men were dead and the treasures were dispersed. Abbot William was succeeded by his nephew, Quintin; a renowned historian, theologian and scholar. Quintin Kennedy was educated at the universities of St Andrews and Paris, a background that would stand him in good stead when he became ambassador for the Regent, Mary of Guise, to the royal courts of England and France in 1554. However, he is best remembered in Carrick history for his momentous three-day debate in Maybole with the formidable John Knox.

In the two years since Parliament had ratified the Reformation of the Church, numerous adherents of both the old and the new forms of worship campaigned, debated and corresponded in support of their respective causes. The climax was reached in the house of the Provost of the College Kirk of Maybole on 28th September, 1562. It came to an inconclusive end but the tide of history was already in Knox's favour. Kennedy died in 1564 after a prolonged illness, thus ending control of the abbey by several generations of the Kennedy family. The new commendator appointed by Queen Mary was Alan Stewart who would almost certainly have been *sib tae a king*. His arrival was not welcomed by the self-styled *King of Carrick*, Gilbert Kennedy, 4th Earl of Cassillis. Stewart was kidnapped in the woods of Crossraguel and taken to Dunure Castle where he was roasted on a spit for three days to force him to sign away the abbey lands to Kennedy. The commendator's account of his torture survives. It is a vivid tale in the Scots language and spares no detail of the terrors he suffered. Sir Walter Scott was suffiently inspired to include a similar scene in his novel *Ivanhoe*.

Quintin Kennedy's debate was part of a very long Scottish tradition of vigorous argument known as *flyting*. It is dramatically displayed in the famous poem, *The Flyting of Dunbar and Kennedy* by William Dunbar (c.1460 – c.1513), one of a band of poets known as *Makars*, the old Scots word for a 'maker' or craftsman. It is in the form of a quarrelsome dialogue packed with scurrilous alliteration and obscentities. The racy narrative focusses on the social, cultural and political conflict between Dunbar's anglophile Lothian and the Gaelic heritage of Carrick of his antagonist, Walter Kennedy of Glen Tig. Little is known of Kennedy's life (although it merits greater enquiry) but what we do learn is that Gaelic was still strong in south-west Scotland at that time. This is a fact attested to by the great George Buchanan (1506 - 1582), a scholar of European stature and a major force during the Reformation.

Buchanan, a humanist and Latin poet who was tutor to Queen Mary and later her son, James VI, spent time at Cassillis House and was tutor to Gilbert Kennedy, the 3rd Earl. It is perhaps through this connection that Buchanan secured a pension from Crossraguel Abbey although he had such difficulties in being paid by David Kennedy of Pennyglen that he sold it on at a loss to the Laird of Bargany, near Girvan.

When James VI succeeded to the Crown of England he arrogantly asserted that he could rule Scotland with 'the stroke of a pen'. But, by declaring Presbyterianism to be incompatible with the monarchy, he set in motion a train of disastrous events that would lead to bloody religious persecution, civil war, the massacre of Glencoe and the genocide of the Highland Clearances after two unsuccessful Jacobite Risings in 1715 and 1745. The king's son and successor, Charles I, imposed the English liturgy on Scotland which provoked the drawing up of the National Covenant in 1638; a solemn affirmation of commitment to the Scottish Presbyterian tradition. It was signed by all classes of people including hundreds from Carrick. Ejected from their kirks, the Presbyterians took to the hills and held secluded worship, baptisms and marriages in gatherings known as conventicles. Ayrshire and Galloway were two strongholds of the Covenanters but also the targets for cruel retribution.

"*The Killing Times*", as this dreadful 50-year period was called, have been well documented. Touching memorials to its martyrs grace the kirkyard of Barr for John Campbell and Edward Keen. There are Covenanter memorials also in the kirkyards of Barrhill (Matthew McIlwraith), Kirkmichael (Gilbert McAdam) and Old Dailly (John Semple and Thomas McClorgan). Near Maybole the Covenanting minister Donald Cargill is commemorated by the place-name Cargilston. A roadside obelisk records a wider story of six Maybole men who perished with more than 200 others in a shipwreck in Orkney as they were being transported into slavery in Barbados. They were Mungo Eccles, Thomas Horn, Robert MacGarron, John McHarrie, John McWhirter and William Roger.

The towering figure of these times was Alexander "*Prophet*" Peden who was born about 1626 in Sorn, Ayrshire. He was hunted relentlessly by British government troops. Such was their wrath that they even dug up his corpse to desecrate it. But Peden's fame and reputation was firmly established to the extent that a thorn tree on Baltersan Mains farm by Maybole, where he preached in the 1660s, was still shown on a map over a hundred years later as an important landmark.

Below: **Kirkmichael**

Below, right: **Old Dailly**

17 HEROES & VILLAINS

"For that is the mark of Scots of all classes; that he stands in an attitude towards the past unthinkable to Englishmen, and remembers and cherishes the memory of his forebears, good and bad; and there burns alive in him a sense of identity with the dead even to the twentieth generation."

Robert Louis Stevenson (1850–1894), *Weir of Hermiston*, 1894

Robert the Bruce: based on a 19th c. portrayal

The passage of time starves logic and feeds romance in such a way that villains become heroes. Robber barons, pirates and smugglers are no longer to be feared so become the stuff of pantomime, children's comics and Hollywood films. But there is a another category of people: those who achieve great things, often from humble beginnings. The greatest historical figure associated with Carrick is, of course, King Robert I (1274-1329), *The Bruce*. Although not from a poor background, he did have to confront enormous challenges in his life as a fugitive, warrior and king. His life is celebrated not just for the re-establishing of Scotland's national sovereignty, but as a glorious example of fortitude in the face of seemingly insurmountable difficulties.

Turnberry lighthouse marks the site of Bruce's castle; the world-famous golf courses there now produce their own heroes, sporting ones.

The individual achiever does not need to come from prosperous circumstances. The German writer Goethe said, "*Talent develops in quiet places, character in the full current of life.*" The tranquillity of early 17th century Colmonell seemed to favour John Snell (1628-1679), the son of a blacksmith. He enrolled at Glasgow University at the age of 14 but did not graduate, leaving after two years. He served in the Royalist

army during the English Civil War and settled in England after the Battle of Worcester in 1651. By 1667 he was an assistant to the Lord Keeper of the Privy Seal and became Seal-bearer. Snell had not forgotten his Scottish university, gifting a valuable collection of books to it in 1661. The following year, he was made a Master of Arts. Other contributions of money were made before his death and his will made provision for Glasgow University students who had studied there for at least a year to receive an education at Baliol College, Oxford, with the first four admitted in 1699. The most famous of the "Snell exhibitioners", as they were called, was the economist, Adam Smith.

Another Carrick student of Glasgow University was James Dalrymple (1619–1695), later 1st Viscount Stair. He became Scotland's most distinguished jurist. His treatise, *The Institutions of the Law of Scotland*, formed the foundations of modern Scots law. Born at Drummurchie in the parish of Barr, Dalrymple served in the army opposed to Charles I during the Bishops' Wars. He practised as an advocate until 1657 when he was appointed a judge. In 1681 he went into a seven-year exile in The Netherlands and returned in the entourage of William, Prince of Orange. Two years later he was elevated to the peerage as Viscount Stair. His son Sir John, 1st Earl of Stair (1648-1707) took on the role of making King William acceptable to the Scots following the deposing of James VII. Stair is primarily remembered for instigating the Massacre of Glencoe. A tradition, worthy of further research, is that a young ensign in the regiment that carried out the massacre was Archibald Kennedy of Maybole who refused to participate in the action. He could have been a kinsman of Lieutenant Gilbert Kennedy who, with Lt Francis Farquhar, broke their swords rather than carry out their orders. They were arrested and imprisoned but later exonerated and released; they then gave evidence for the prosecution against their superior officers.

An earlier resident of Drummurchie at the beginning of the 17th century was Thomas Kennedy, brother to the Laird of Bargany. He was entangled in the protracted feud between the Kennedys of Cassillis and Bargany and, as a result, he was found guilty of treason in 1604. He forfeited all his property for the burning of the house of Auchensoul, near Barr. This bloodfeud, a well-documented series of *tit-for-tat* actions and reactions, led to the death of the young Laird of Bargany at a conflict between 80 of his supporters and 200 followers of the Earl of Cassillis at Brockloch, outside Maybole, in December, 1601. The now outdated sense of "romance" of this evil period, fostered by kailyard writers such as S.R. Crockett, has at times overshadowed other Carrick men and women who have made important contributions to life, not just in their homeland, but in the wider world. One such was Sir Gilbert Blane (1749–1834) who was born at Blanefield in the parish of Kirkoswald. Having taken the degree of Medical Doctor at Glasgow University in 1778, he went on to become Physician to the Fleet in the West Indies during the American War of Independence. During that period he discovered a method, using lime juice, of combating scurvy, common among sailors at the time during long voyages. Commanding the Fleet was Lord Rodney, who said of Blane, *"To [his] knowledge and attention it was owing that the English Fleet [sic] was, notwithstanding their excessive fatigue and constant service, in a condition always to attack and defeat the public enemy. In my own ship, the 'Formidable', out of 900 men, not one was buried in six months."* Blane became one of the physicians to King George IV and also to his successor, William IV.

By coincidence the name Rodney connects Blane's naval exploits to another notable Carrick man, Admiral Sir Frederick Dalrymple-Hamilton of Bargany. He was captain of HMS. Rodney at the stalking and sinking of the German battleship Bismarck on 27th May, 1941. His gunnery officer that day was his nephew, William Crawford, from New Zealand, where Sir Bernard Fergusson (1911-1980), Baron Ballantrae of Auchairne, became Governor General in the footsteps of his father and grandfather.

Another member of the family, Sir James, the 8th baronet (1904-1973) was keeper of the Records of Scotland from 1949 to 1969 as well as an author of several works on Carrick's history.

Bargany monument, Ballantrae: an elaborate Renaissance tomb for Gilbert Kennedy, the young Laird of Bargany, killed at the battle of Brockloch, near Maybole in 1601. He was involved in a feud with the Kennedys of Cassillis. His death ultimately led to the decline of this once-powerful branch of the Kennedy name. The Laird and his Lady had originally been interred at St John's Kirk in Ayr. Their bodies were brought to Ballantrae in an impressive cortege accompanied by *"a thousand gentlemen on horseback"*. (*Private, not open to the public*)

Revd John Thomson, of Duddingston, Edinburgh: self portrait, oil on millboard, 1816.
Born in the parish of Dailly, Carrick in 1778.

Image reproduced courtesy of South Ayrshire Council

Jane Kennedy and Agnes Broun are two women from opposite ends of the social spectrum whose lives touched upon two of Scotland's most famous people – Mary, Queen of Scots, and Robert Burns. Attending Mary at her execution were her two favourite ladies-in-waiting, Jane Kennedy from Carrick and Elizabeth Curle. According to a 19th century account, Jane was involved in another dramatic act in the Queen's life when Mary escaped from Loch Leven Castle. In the confusion of the escape Jane was left behind but was determined to catch up. Miss Strickland, the author of the (dubious) account, wrote:

"Jane Kennedy, her other damsel who was to have accompanied her, not being quick enough to reach the outer gate till they were locked by the retreating party, leaped from the Queen's chamber window into the Loch, and striking out, swam stoutly after the boat till she overtook it, and was received into that little ark."

Agnes Broun (1732-1820) on the other hand, did nothing more dangerous than attend a fair in Maybole in 1756 where she met William Burnes and fell in love. They were married in the town on 15th December, 1757. Just over a year later, they had a son, Robert Burns (1759-1795). The rest, as they say, is history. Agnes was born at Craigenton Farm, Kirkoswald, and the village was to feature later in the Bard's life as the place where he received his schooling.

Revd John Thomson (1778-1840), of Duddingston, knew how to escape *to* his tower. His painting studio was in a building which he called *Edinburgh* and if he did not want to be disturbed by visitors his wife simply told them: "*He's in Edinburgh*". Thomson was born in Dailly, where he became the minister in 1800. The youngest of four sons, John was taught Greek and Latin by his brother Thomas, a brilliant scholar who became a distinguished lawyer. While studying theology John took up an interest in painting, taking lessons from the great landscape artist and portraitist, Alexander Nasmyth. After five years as minister at Dailly, where his father and grandfather had

Top:
Thomson Tower, Duddingston, the octagonal building used as a studio

Bottom:
Dailly parish church

also been ministers, he left for Duddingston in Edinburgh. His classical education allowed him to mix freely with, and befriend, the cream of Edinburgh society which included Sir Walter Scott and renowned scientist Sir David Brewster. With a passion for painting, Thomson mixed in artistic circles and influenced younger painters such as Horatio McCulloch and William Bell Scott (later of Penkill fame). In 1818 Sir Walter Scott collaborated with Thomson and the great English artist, Joseph Mallord William Turner, on a book entitled *The Provincial Antiquities of Scotland.*

With a busy social life and an established reputation as an artist, Thomson seems to have been inattentive in his parochial duties, but he was known to have been generous in attending to people's material needs. He enjoyed life to the full and the proximity of Duddingston Loch gave him the opportunity to indulge his passion for curling. The first laws of curling were laid down by the Duddingston Curling Society in 1806. Thomson, though, was not the skating minister on Duddingston Loch featured in the iconic painting attributed to Sir Henry Raeburn. That was a contemporary, Revd David Walker.

Thomson is most affectionately remembered in a phrase of all-embracing brotherhood. He and his second wife both had children from their first marriages. To those were added a third set of children which caused people to ask who belonged to whom. The simple answer became that famous saying: *"We are all Jock Tamson's bairns"*.

Slavery was still legal in the British Empire in Thomson's day so he would not have been surprised to know the story of black servant Scipio Kennedy in early-18th century Culzean. At the time there was a slave ship named *Scipio* after which the boy was possibly named. His life in Scotland was vastly different to what he left behind as he was given a cottage and land on the estate. He was rebuked on 9th June, 1728, by Kirkoswald Kirk Session, along with Jean Fergusson, for "scandals". In October that year he married Margaret Gray, who was pregnant with their first child. They subsequently had seven other children. Scipio and Margaret took up weaving linen and cotton goods. But he was not the only black servant in Ayrshire. Among others was Robert Campbell from Jamaica, butler to A.W. Hamilton, of Pinmore, for 50 years. Campbell died at Belleisle, Ayr, in 1838. The Hamilton family owned a number of slave plantations in Jamaica. Pinmore House was destroyed by fire in 1876 but later rebuilt.

Two Carrick characters whose images are immortalised in stone are Tam o Shanter and Souter Johnnie. Although fictional, they are based on real people. For his famous narrative poem, Robert Burns chose Douglas Graham, a smuggler and tenant farmer at Shanter, near Turnberry. His drinking crony, the souter (shoemaker), was inspired by John Davidson who had his cobbler's workshop in a cottage on Main Street, Kirkoswald. A self-taught Ayrshire sculptor, James Thom, created life-size statues of the two men around 1830, along with the innkeeper and the innkeeper's wife. They are now housed in the alehouse behind the workshop which is now known as Souter Johnnie's cottage. Both buildings are maintained by the National Trust for Scotland.

For some, fame emerges from a quiet, modest life dedicated to a talent and a passion. James Smith tenanted two acres at Monkwood, Minishant, where he established a botanical garden with 2,000 hardy exotics plus British specimens and 500 varieties of greenhouse plants. He achieved recognition as one of Scotland's leading botanists and was a founder member of the Ayrshire Horticultural Society in 1815.

A woman at the opposite end of the social spectrum from Kirkton Jean was heiress, Elsie Mackay (1893-1928), daughter of shipping magnate, Lord Inchcape of Glen App. An actress, Elsie, whose stage name was Poppy Whyndam, was a pioneer aviator fascinated by the race to become the first woman to fly the Atlantic Ocean. Accompanied by Walter Hinchcliffe in a single-engine plane, she set off in wintry conditions from Grantham in Lincolnshire in March, 1928. They were lost without trace.

Pinmore House about five miles south-east of Girvan

The following year saw the death of a man more famous in Lafayette, Indiana, than his native Carrick. Thomas Duncan (1865-1929) was born at Drumranny, a farm to the north-east of Girvan. The son of a ploughman, Thomas showed an early interest in science and as a schoolboy set up some frightening experiments at home. At the age of 17 he emigrated to Boston, Massachussets, and found work with the Sun Electrical Company. His determination to pursue his interest in electrical development led him to take up a job at one-eighth of his previous salary. His pioneering work with electric meters led to him securing his first patent and in 1901 he established the Duncan Electric Manufacturing Company in Lafayette, employing 500 people to meet the global demand for his products. He is regarded as the founder of the electric meter industry in the USA and his company now trades as Landis & Gyr.

From an equally humble background in Girvan came Roderick Lawson (1831-1907), son of a rope spinner. He was destined to become a Presbyterian minister in Maybole—a post he held for 34 years until 1897. Immensely energetic and, as he would describe himself, a compulsive "scribbler", Lawson plunged into the life of the town which then had chronic social problems. The weaving industry had died but boot and shoe manufacture had scarcely begun. His first career as a teacher saw him overcome challenges that would have deterred weaker men. When he discovered his pupils had no grammar or geography textbooks, he wrote them himself. That trait of practical solutions stood him in good stead for the ministry. He was called by the West Kirk of Maybole in 1863.

Maybole Castle

Lawson, who never married, was as distressed by the prevalence of irregular marriages or "handfasting" in the town, as he was with the poverty and illiteracy that was endemic. The man's activities and achievements are legendary in Carrick. He was more than a mere "scribbler", for his written works and his beloved practical solutions have bestowed upon future generations a valuable account of his life and times. Although well-known locally, Revd Lawson merits a wider audience for his life's work.

Another man with Girvan connections , albeit in a completely different world from that of Duncan and Lawson, is Alex Cubie, an illustrator for the *Rupert the Bear* strip cartoon in the Daily Express. Cubie's work from 1974 to 1977 was noted for the use of stronger lines and more vibrant colours than his predecessor, Alfred Bestall.

At a different part of the cultural spectrum are two very interesting, and yet scarcely recorded, Carrick men. Robert Finnie McEwen, a solicitor and art lover, inherited a not insubstantial sum of money and built Bardrochat House. He and his friend, David Conn, headmaster of Colmonell School until 1917, were classics scholars; one spoke Greek, the other, Latin. They alternated social visits to each other's houses and when in one, they conversed in Greek and in the other, they spoke Latin.

Their story though, is not exceptional in Carrick. For some, education was bought. For others, the self-taught, like Lang Sandy, the fossil collector, Thomas Duncan, the inventor or Roderick Lawson, the dynamic teacher and minster, it was gained by a stubborn determination to improve oneself. And in the process, to improve the lives of those around them. In braid Scots (which still flourishes in Carrick), they were *thrawn lads o pairts*.

Whether the sons and daughters of ploughmen, blacksmiths or barons, Carrick has bred many interesting characters, some of whose stories have been told here, if only fleetingly. Everyone has a tale to tell and beyond Carrick there is a ready audience. Thanks to the many story-tellers in every community in the region, this book will widen that audience for it has gone beyond the guide books into the cherished memories of the kind of people Robert Louis Stevenson had in mind in the quotation at the beginning of this chapter. The story has just begun and the enquiring mind will want to know more. ❑

'THE ELECTRIC BRAE'

KNOWN LOCALLY AS 'CROY BRAE'

THIS RUNS THE QUARTER MILE FROM THE BEND
OVERLOOKING CROY RAILWAY VIADUCT
IN THE WEST (286 FEET ABOVE ORDNANCE DATUM)
TO THE WOODED CRAIGENCROY GLEN
(303 FEET A.O.D.) TO THE EAST.
WHILST THERE IS THIS SLOPE OF 1 IN 86
UPWARDS FROM THE BEND TO THE GLEN,
THE CONFIGURATION OF THE LAND
ON EITHER SIDE OF THE ROAD
PROVIDES AN OPTICAL ILLUSION,
MAKING IT LOOK AS IF
THE SLOPE IS GOING THE OTHER WAY.
THEREFORE, A STATIONARY CAR
ON THE ROAD WITH THE BRAKES OFF
WILL APPEAR TO MOVE SLOWLY UPHILL.
THE TERM 'ELECTRIC' DATES FROM A TIME
WHEN IT WAS INCORRECTLY THOUGHT
TO BE A PHENOMENON CAUSED BY ELECTRIC
OR MAGNETIC ATTRACTION WITHIN THE BRAE

Electric Brae
This is surely the quirkiest feature of
Carrick. On 26th August, 1930, while
staying at Kilkerran, the English
writer of ghost stories, **Montague
Rhodes James** (1862-1936), wrote,
*"On Sunday p.m. by the way drove out to
what they call Magnetic Hill, which is a
most puzzling stretch of road skirting a
hill: you could swear it sloped down-
wards, yet when the car is stopped it
begins to run backwards uphill, optical
illusion of course, but impossible to detect
why, or what the catch is."*

This stone (*left*), at a lay-by on the
A719 coast road, midway between
Fisherton and Culzean Castle, gives a
full explanation.

Acknowledgements

Many people in Carrick have freely given of their time to contribute to the writing of this book. Others have willingly supplied photographs, leaflets, books and written notes on topics for which they have a passion. That made my job both easier and harder. Easier in that it pointed the way to very useful research. Harder in that the volume of material went well beyond the capacity of this book to cover in depth. Every community council area was visited and there are too many to name all individually. But, some people made particularly valuable contributions and I wish to thank them. They are:

The publication group of David Kiltie, Charles Ellis, Keith and Beryl Dawdry who gently guided me (and the content of the book) after their unenviable task of reading the rough drafts.

Beryl Dawdry at The Pottery, Pinmore *www.peinnmor.co.uk* who supplied the exceptional iconic line drawings for the opening of each chapter and background illustrations for each of the four main topics. The drawings add a delightful personal touch that could not have been achieved by any other means.

My wife, Susi Cormack Brown, for proofreading and guidance on book production.

Stuart Lindsay (*Ailsa Horizons Ltd*) and the committee of Carrick Community Councils' Forum for their practical support and encouragement.

I am also grateful for the support as well as the local and specialist knowledge of:

Dr David Anderson, Michael Ansell, Kathryn Baldwin, John Craig, Jim Cuthbertson, Catherine Czerkawska, John Douglas, James Farquhar, Auriole Fergusson, Neil Gregory, John Jackson, Ian Jones, Roddy Leitch, Keith Brown, Hew McCallum, Margaret McCance, Jean McGarva, John McGarva, John McIlwraith, Jimmy McLauchlin, Jessie Milroy, Drew Moyes, Alec Oattes, Rich Petit, Denis Rattenbury, Denis Reid, Beverley Ross, Stephen Scholes, Bob Stewart, Roy Storie, Alistair Wallace, John Wilson, Robert Wright, Winifred Wright and the staff of Carrick Academy and Girvan Academy.

Picture Credits

In addition to attributed illustrations, images have been supplied by the author and others. I am grateful to Girvan Camera Club for many fine photographs (pages 27, 30, 54, 55, 74, 78, 79 and 96).

James Brown, 2009

Postscript

This is not the end, but a new beginning, with suggestions on the following pages.

To capture the essence of the ancient earldom of Carrick is no easy task. The scope of this publication looks at four main components of the fabric of the region which have created a distinctive culture. That culture has, in turn, been shaped by the great geological forces which created Carrick. The hills and valleys have formed the distinctive flora and fauna we enjoy today. But, in months of research and meeting people in every community council area in the region, it is the history which fires the blood. History is a country's memory. Much of what appears on the pages of this book was prompted by knowledgeable, caring people in every community in Carrick. They sowed the seeds which the author has cultivated.

Scotland is one of the most linguistically diverse places in Europe and Carrick shares that distinction. It shows in the fascinating place-names with origins in Gaelic, Cumbric, Anglo-Saxon and Scots. These places speak of the types of landscape and soils the early farmers had to contend with. The plethora of saints' names tells us of the deep spirituality of Carrick. Much is known, or should be better known. And yet, much is still to be learned. Some things are not destined to be world-famous such as the history of boat building at Maidens or the enterprising jam factory in Barr. But they are of value, for they inform us of an industrious people, each with a story to tell.

The limited space available in this book has allowed only an introduction to the many and varied facets of Carrick, its culture and people. But in its breadth it goes beyond the tourist guides and invites further exploration.

Grass of Parnassus
© Harriet Ellis

Looking deeper, learning more

One of the purposes of this book is to sow the seeds of curiosity in each community in Carrick. Is there, for example, an economic benefit to be gained from a deeper and wider knowledge of the region? The following pages contain just a few suggestions that could form the basis of future studies and co-operative actions.

Family history:
Scotland is the best country in the world for re-searching family history. How can those who are tracing family trees in Carrick be helped? Is it time to look again at Carrick's monumental in-scriptions? (Originally published by The Scottish Genealogy Society in 1997: ISBN 0 901061 34 4).

18th c. headstone
Barr Kirkyard

George Ingram:
Girvan's oldest lifeboatman at 68 years

© Newsquest (Herald & Times). Licensor www.scran.ac.uk

92

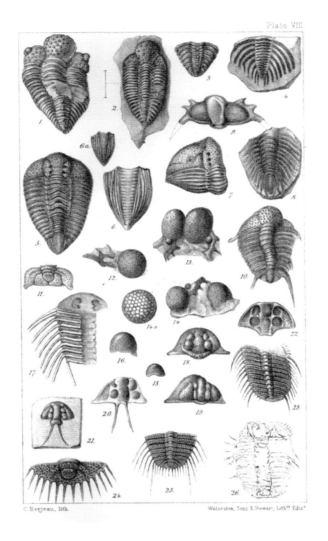

Fossil collections:
Fossils from the Girvan area are world-famous and yet collections of them are in storage in various places outwith Carrick.

Is it possible they could be brought "home"?

Milestones:
These are a significant reminder of the days of coaches and horses. They are part of the character of Carrick.

Is there mileage in restoring Carrick's milestones?

Further Reading

Much of the information on moths and butterflies has been taken from a paper by Richard Sutcliffe: *Recent changes in the distribution of some Scottish butterflies and the arrival of new species in Scotland* Published in *The Glasgow Naturalist*, (2009) Volume 25, Part 2, 5-12

Recommended websites:

http://www.southwestscotland-butterflies.org.uk
http://www.ayrshire-birding.org.uk
http://www.agatesofscotland.co.uk
http://www.maybole.org

Girvan Fossils is a 48-page, full-colour booklet from which information for this book has been gleaned. It is extensive in its coverage of the subject and includes beautiful photographs by Colin Blane and Jed Connelly.

Written by Mark Hope with other contributors Published by Friends of the McKechnie Institute, Girvan

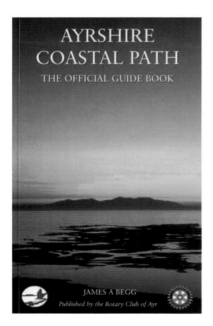

Ayrshire Coastal Paths is a wonderful book for all who enjoy wildlife, fresh air, scenery, rambling or simply strolling. It is packed with information in a neat, clear format.

ISBN 978-0-9559063-0-5
Written by James Begg
Published by the Rotary Club of Ayr

Opposite:
View towards Culzean Castle with Ailsa Craig on the horizon
© Alister G. Firth

Varyag memorial

The early-20th c. Russian battle cruiser *Varyag* is a cultural icon in that country. By 1920 it was sold as a hulk and, *en route* to Germany, it ran aground off Lendalfoot and sank. The memorial was unveiled on 30th July, 2006.

Do Carrick's older memorials need the loving care of a new *Old Mortality*?

Old Stumpy, Girvan
It is a well-known landmark, but how well-known is the story behind it?